The 7 Strategies of Highly Successful Business Owners

Second Edition

By Jacob M Hanes

Revised second edition published 2019
First published 2016
Printed in the United States of America

Requests for permission should be directed to:
The Corporate Legal Team
Action Tax Service, LLC
1833 Auburn Way N, Ste T
Auburn, WA 98002 USA.

"I first met Jacob Hanes at a special invitation-only coaching event I held in Seattle, Washington in conjunction with a few of my franchise business coaches and their top-performing clients. As a client of ActionCOACH Kevin Weir, Mr. Hanes was on his third successful business venture at the time and living the dream of a true entrepreneur. This was just a year after the horrific economic recession that hit the world in 2008. But even that hasn't slowed his progress. A man after my own first love (accounting, can you believe it?), Mr. Hanes has written a well-researched book that draws upon his many experiences as a business owner and community leader. His expertise as a Certified Public Accountant is clearly evident. Now, he has launched a truly inspiring website, www.smallbizzoom.com, and has authored his second book. It is great to see him continue to thrive and grow. Readers can expect to find a plethora of business-changing resources within this book. I was honored to be asked to write the foreword to *The 7 Strategies of Highly Successful Business Owners* and I highly recommend it to both seasoned and burgeoning entrepreneurs."

Brad Sugars, Founder and CEO of ActionCOACH GLOBAL

"Effective, honest, straight forward, practical, interesting, meaningful, true, a fast read, a useful tool, a simply excellent and perhaps even brilliant book. Don't let this pass you up!!! It's full of rich, useful and powerful golden nuggets that will not only improve any business but will improve your personal and family life as well. Read it. Hang on to it. Savor it. Underline it. Use it. Most of all, though, refer to it often. I encourage all people interested in small business, big business, or simply organizing or improving life in general to relish The 7 Strategies of Highly Successful Business Owners."

Laura Kiel, Kiel Mortgage and Radio Personality

"The 7 Strategies of Highly Successful Business Owners is a great go-to resource for any business owner! This book is packed full of tips from saving money on taxes, to building productive teams, increasing sales and much more in an easy to read format. You will get not only all these incredible tools but also an intimate look into the life of a successful business owner himself, Jacob Hanes. I highly recommend this book to anyone whether they're starting out or have been in business for a while."

Catherine M White, Accelerated Results 365
(Consultant & John Maxwell Team coach)

"Jake Hanes has provided some of the most effective, yet simple solutions that any business owner could easily implement immediately into their business. I know it will be mandatory reading for all my clients and it should be mandatory reading for you if you own any type of business."

Kevin Weir, ActionCOACH - Spokane

"Being a small business owner myself, always overrun with work to keep current in my own industry, I appreciate the simple, easy-to-grasp way in which this book is written. I'm so encouraged, it is not "Rocket Science." Practical steps I can take with resources I can use to increase my productivity by 'working smarter not harder!' Excellent material, a very valuable and important read for anyone running a small business!"

Andrea Villanueva, InnerNet Sales & Consulting

Contents

The information provided in this book and any accompanying material is for informational purposes only. It should not be considered legal or financial advice. You should consult with an attorney or other professional to determine what may be best for your individual needs. I make no guarantee or promise as to any results that may be obtained from applying any of the contents of this book. No one should make any investment decision without first consulting his financial advisor as well as conducting his own research and due diligence. To the maximum extent permitted by law, I disclaim any and all liability in the event that any information, commentary, analysis, opinion, advice or recommendation proves to be inaccurate, incomplete or unreliable, or result in any investment or other losses. I am also not responsible for the content or links to other internet sites or resources that I may refer to. These are the property or copyright of third party owners and you use it at your own risk. The content, accuracy, opinions expressed and any other external links provided at these websites are not investigated, verified, modified or endorsed by me.

The content herein is not intended to and does not constitute legal or investment advice. Your use of any information here is at your own risk. While special care has been taken in preparing the information and materials in this book, such information and materials are provided to you on an "as-is" basis and carry no warranty or representation of any kind, express or implied.

Foreword

It was 30 years ago that I first met Jake Hanes. At the time, I was serving as a Varsity Scout leader in Olympia, WA, providing high adventure and leadership experiences for young men. My hope was to impart some practical 'woods wisdom' to these impressionable youth, helping them to gain a lifelong appreciation for the outdoors while guiding their understanding of leading a principled life.

Serving with youth can bring great satisfaction but the greater payday comes later in life, when those whom you served are now serving others in their community, running successful businesses, raising great families and exhibiting their citizenship in the community, if you will, making a truly positive impact.

One of those young scouts has continued to cross my life's path and each of those encounters has brought enriching experiences and memories. Jake was no ordinary young man. He was born with innate business savvy, coupled with an impressive personal drive.

As a teenager, with money he earned from odd jobs, he bought a lawnmower which he then pushed around the neighborhood building a fledgling lawn care service. When he had collected enough funds to purchase a car, he expanded his business, investing in more equipment while also saving for his future education and life plans.

Jake was not only a self-starter but he was also the youngest self-actualized person I ever met. He knew what he wanted to accomplish and was driven to do so. He never hesitated or looked back.

I also took note that early on, he grasped the vision of serving others and even provided some financial assistance to those in need, even when it presented some personal sacrifice on his part.

When he was about 17, he shared with me some entries on his list of 100 things he wanted to accomplish at that time in his life. One such entry he hoped to accomplish would require my assistance.

So he presented what he hoped to do - summit Mt. Rainier before his 19th birthday. Together we did so, creating one of the most memorable experiences of my life. He now leads climbs of his own, and last year, he joined me on a climb to Camp Muir in my 60th year.

He continues to create lists of things he intends to accomplish, including the writing of this book. *The 7 Strategies of Highly Successful Business Owners* may be the most interesting, yet informative, book for small business owners available.

It's filled with practical ways to grow your bottom line, from the perspective of a CPA who has taken the time to share key principles to achieve maximum results. I think you will find it's no ordinary read but one worth every minute of the time you invest to grow your business and take it to the next level.

Bill George

Acknowledgments

Thank you to the many leaders throughout my life who have inspired and challenged me to reach higher and to be a better leader.

Thank you to my business coach, Kevin Weir, who not only helped me turn my first CPA firm into a highly successful business but continues to support me in achieving my vision. His knowledge, friendship, and contributions to my success are the reasons I am able to write this book today.

Thank you to all of my teammates at my CPA firm. Each person on my team has indirectly contributed to this book by freeing up my time to write and edit it. I have had the privilege of working with many fabulous, powerful and dedicated individuals. It makes going to the office a joy.

Thank you to Rowena Morais for her hundreds of insights in editing this book. Her contributions and her professional experience make a contribution to this book that cannot be calculated.

Thank you to my wife and family, who always keep me grounded and make life a joy beyond measure.

Introduction

As the door opened and I stepped into the limo, laying my head back, I let out a soft sigh of relief. It was done and now it was a reality.

I was now the owner of a multi-million dollar business. Little did I know, this moment would soon leapfrog me to the next level and put me on the path to achieving success far beyond my wildest dreams.

While nothing in my life had come easy, and my humble beginnings always kept me grounded in reality, I took a moment to reflect on the series of events that had gotten me here. Nothing on the list is what you could call positive, but somehow, it all worked out.

First, a whirlwind of public relations nightmares. Then, the loss and departure of a key team member, followed by a series of unexpected economic setbacks that created a lot of turmoil for me leading up to this day.

But here I was and I could scarcely believe that, at this moment, I had succeeded in achieving a huge milestone in my life and career.

Just as I began to relax, another thought hit me. Now the real hard work begins. I thought to myself, "Brad, if you think the journey getting here was hard, just wait till tomorrow!"

I understood, at that moment, that it was my responsibility to take the lead with this newly purchased company, put processes and systems in place to make it run effectively and build a team with the right people who could achieve all the new goals before us. I remember thinking, "well if your dreams don't scare you a little, they aren't big enough."

Running a business of any size, in any industry, can be like riding a roller coaster. The only difference is that you can't (or shouldn't be able to) crash while on a roller coaster. But, oh, you sure can in business.

The great highs and the tragic lows faced in running any business enterprise can test your character and endurance. It is, however, the rewards, some small some big, that make running a truly successful business worth the journey.

I am Brad Sugars, founder and CEO of ActionCOACH, a business coaching company, serving more than 18,000 businesses globally every week, helping them improve their bottom line. I now have nearly 1,000 coaches in more than 70 countries and we are projected to be in 120 countries by 2025.

In 1993, I started ActionCOACH alone and created not only a company - I created an industry. You see, business coaching wasn't a thing back then. There was no road map. In 1997, when I awarded my first franchise, I knew that we were on to something huge.

Today, ActionCOACH is the undisputed leader in the business coaching industry both domestically and internationally. Sustaining dominance for more than 25 years now means that the products, services, and resources we offer our franchise partners and our coaches continue to be vital to businesses of all sizes.

Coaches work with owners to achieve basic business objectives and reach new levels of success and achievement every day, with the strategies and systems ActionCOACH has perfected.

It has always been my belief that, as a business owner, you need a team to help you succeed. I believe every business owner needs to hire an accountant, a lawyer **and** a certified business coach to ensure all their bases are covered. These key team members are only the tip of the iceberg though. You need to consider your other stakeholders as you navigate the complexities of running a highly successful business.

Finding the right resources is just as important as having the right employees, choosing the best vendors and creating the best strategic alliances so that you can provide the best customer service and return on investment to all your stakeholders.

Hiring a certified business coach is a great first step but every entrepreneur needs to continue to educate themselves.

This book, *The 7 Strategies of Highly Successful Business Owners,* is a great resource. It will provide you with insight on creating the best team and implementing the most effective strategies to grow your enterprise.

No matter your age, the industry you're in, or your current level of success in business to date, this book will provide the practical resources, insights, best practices, and ultimately, a step-by-step roadmap to put your business on the road to high-level success and maximum growth.

Mr. Hanes, who has personally worked with one of our certified and award-winning business coaches, Kevin Weir of ActionCOACH, has one of the most successful businesses in his own industry. He has been working with a coach for more than 15 years.

He is now sharing his knowledge and real-world experience using the ActionCOACH vision of "creating world abundance through business re-education".

The strategies he shares with you in this book, *The 7 Strategies of Highly Successful Business Owners,* will help you have a more predictable cash flow, help you better leverage your resources and help you deal with the economic uncertainty and volatility of today's changing marketplace.

Mr. Hanes shares candid true stories to help you discover:

- the best ways to effectively increase revenues through customer acquisition and nurturing;
- the strategies from the world's top experts on how to market your business successfully;
- simple-to-follow core principles on how to streamline your business;

- the fastest ways to manage cash flows;
- the 5 key strategies to be an effective leader in business today;
- the #1 thing to avoid in order to be truly successful in business;
- the process for hiring the right people and building a powerful team;
- and ways to create a highly profitable business that runs without you.

As a business owner, it is important to look at your business through a different lens and open your eyes to new possibilities. Whether you are new to business, or a seasoned professional, as you read these pages, take the time to look at your business through the eyes of a business coach.

Be your own coach for a moment. Be an objective observer who can provide honest insight to help your business become more effective. Think of this book and the resources contained inside as a roadmap to navigate the business terrain ahead.

Make a plan, map out a strategy and consider the options you have to get you to your desired destination.

My road has been uniquely my own but it has never been **on my own**. I continue to add to my toolkit of skills, add to my knowledge base and continue to be a student of business so that I can stay ahead of my competition.

As entrepreneurs, we are all masters of our fate but we should never isolate ourselves and think we have nothing left to learn. As you continue on your journey, use the knowledge you get from this great book to help you navigate a smoother course.

You also might consider getting a business coach to help you chart the future. Remember "the biggest mistake you can make is to do nothing at all".

Brad Sugars

Brad Sugars, Founder & CEO
ActionCOACH° Global
The #1 Business Coaching Franchise in the World.

"If success was easy, everyone would be doing it."

Give Yourself More Take-Home Pay

Build a strong foundation that protects
your money and prevents unnecessary loss

1| What's Better Than A Tax Deduction?

Generating income and claiming all those credits

They say money can't buy happiness. I say give me 100 dollars, you can watch me smile

–Anonymous

One of my favorite clients, Shelly, is the owner of a small architectural firm and she happens to be a wonderful lady and friend to all of my staff. She was sitting at my desk one day, feverishly waiting on my final review of her tax returns so that she would know just how much she owed Uncle Sam.

MAKING MONEY THIS YEAR

Over the past two years, we had worked hard together to tackle three enormous tasks, that blossomed her business (which I'll not only share with you in this book but show you how to do yourself). The results had been fabulous.

Shelly was in a good place financially, after hard work and coaching, but she also knew the implications of going from a loss in her business in the previous year to making some money this year.

She sat there patiently as I slowly and methodically focused on producing the best possible results for her. There were two occasions when she asked me, with a tinge of fear in her voice, what her tax bill would look like this year.

The first time I answered her, I took my eyes off the computer screen and looked her straight in the eye, replying softly, "You are going to owe this year, of course, but I'm looking at a few more possible deductions we might be able to take advantage of."

"Good," she responded, "You make sure you find me every deduction possible. I just can't believe after slaving so much this past year and I finally make a little profit that the IRS just takes it!"

Time went by slowly and after a few more minutes, the pressure got to be too much. She asked me another question and was not prepared for the answer given.

"What?" she cried out in a near panic. "How in the world could that be? Oh no, Jake, how am I supposed to pay that?" Her fear was palpable.

A NEAR FATAL ERROR

It was only after I looked up and saw her face that I realized something was wrong. I quickly replayed the scene in my mind and then it hit me. I was looking at the net income of her business while she was asking me about how much she would owe the IRS. I had shot my answer off quickly, "Looks like about $61,912, Shelly. Nice job! "

Ha!

Our strategies saved her over $12,000 on that single day.

I was talking about her income but she was talking about her taxes. Luckily, I quickly caught this near-fatal error and explained myself. The anxiety and fearful intensity melted away as we burst out in uncontrolled laughter! As it turned out, I had some pretty good news - Shelly would only owe the IRS $2,311! But let me share her backstory.

The year Shelly was referred to our firm, she had been in business for just three years. She started out with a touch of luck and a great connection. Armed with a contract that gave her instant, good income, she was able to thrive for those first two years, producing fabulous results.

Her profit in the second year soared to just over $78,000 but bad advice and a "commission paid tax preparer" at the local tax office quickly ate into her numbers. She was told she owed the IRS just under $16,000! In sheer desperation, she called her friend, a long-time client of our firm, who quickly got her in to meet me. Our strategies saved her over $12,000 on that single day.

Needless to say, it was tremendously great news for her not only because she did not have $16,000 but she had just lost her big contract. That coupled with the bad economy in 2009 would have meant the end of her practice.

THE RIGHT CHOICE

You're probably wondering why one tax preparer can give you one tax liability while another can get a completely different result? How am I, with more than 2,000 clients now, able to sit down with my clients and so quickly identify where and when they have overpaid the IRS needlessly?

Yes, the tax code is complex. Yes, there are more than 75,000 pages of methodically prepared jargon and minutiae weaving in and out of those regulations, directives and forms that make up the tax system which ultimately forms the bankrolls of government income. Yet with your welfare in mind, we the experts, are able to whittle all of that down and turn it into income, deductions, more deductions and credits (and I just love those credits!).

In this book, I share with you the best and most overlooked credits. You will also get a better understanding of deductions which, whether due to lack of knowledge or fear, you and many others, do not take advantage of.

My question to you is this. What is the only thing better than a tax credit (speaking in terms of taxes, that is)? More income, of course. I will share with you, more than 300 ways of generating revenue, along with a list of the only six things that are not tax-deductible for anyone. And no, your pet is not on the list! But first, I'd like to share another story with you.

2 | Why Isn't Everyone Doing It?

What it is and why you need to incorporate your business this way

*Incorporating your business could be the biggest
tax-saving strategy you ever use*

–Jacob M Hanes

It was the spring of 2001. I had just completed another tax season as a fairly new tax practitioner and was happy to get a much-needed break from the grueling hours involved. One fine morning in mid-April, I met with one of my new clients, a landscaper, at her request. She needed my help to determine her upcoming tax bill. When I shared the estimates with her (it was more than $18,000 estimated for the year), she just would not accept it.

"Jake," she said matter-of-factly, "You need to look into setting me up in such a way that I don't pay so much money to the IRS. I mean, this is just unfair. It's wrong!"

I spent fifteen minutes, explaining how I understood that it was a lot but then I also shared some advice about things she could do to lower her taxes (such as spending a lot more money on IRAs, etc). She listened patiently but was undeterred in her resolve. I had to find a way to lower her burden drastically.

> "You know, young man, if that were possible, our former CPA would have told us about it long ago," one of the partners retorted.

Ironically, it was only a few years ago that I was almost exactly in her shoes! At that time, I was the owner of a small landscaping business and was staring at a tax bill that made me squirm. It really hit me deep to have to pay so much tax on top of what I felt was the terribly high cost the landscaping business incurred.

In the end, I had to leave my entrepreneurial dreams aside and get back into private accounting for a few more miserable years. Thinking back over our conversations though, one thing she said resonated with me. She said that there had to be a way to minimize the enormous tax bill she had as a small business owner.

She was dealing with a 15.3 percent self-employment tax as well as a 15 percent federal income tax. There had to be a way to cut or reduce that 30.3 percent slice into her cash flow. I knew I had to dig deeper. I studied whatever resources were available (there was not much online in 2001 but there were great tax books to read) and I learned that if you are a corporation, you could avoid paying self-employment tax. That is the nasty 15.3 percent tax on the net income of your business. I had to find out more!

WHAT ARE S CORPORATIONS?

S Corporations are corporations that elect to pass corporate income, losses, deductions and credits through to their shareholders for federal tax purposes. Shareholders of S Corporations report the flow-through of income and losses on their personal tax returns and are assessed tax at their individual income tax rates.

This allows S Corporations to avoid double taxation on the corporate income. S Corporations are responsible for tax on certain built-in gains and passive income at the entity level.

https://www.irs.gov/businesses/small-businesses-self-employed/s-corporations

For three weeks, I studied tax laws that applied to corporations. Then, I called the IRS but that didn't help much. Oddly enough, I seemed to know more than they did. I kept at it, learning more as I went along and then, about a month later, I succeeded in helping my client set herself up as a Corporation, an S Corporation to be exact.

It didn't take long for the entrepreneur in me to realize that I was on to something big! I had found the goose that lays the golden eggs. Every business that I could possibly reach had to hear this immediately!

That was 2001. Over the next fifteen years and more, my firm would go on to help literally thousands incorporate their businesses, saving them collectively, millions of dollars!

Here's another example worth sharing. In 2003, as my tax practice began to flourish, I met with the three partners of an engineering firm. They each had different personal tax preparers but were looking to hire me to prepare their partnership tax return.

I completed their initial return, which due to their combined profits of $315,000 (shared equally) meant that they were each incurring a tax bill of more than $16,000 just in self-employment tax. They begrudgingly agreed that this was something they were stuck with, and wanting to escape reality, they were all ready to get out the door to get a beer.

Stopping them, I was eager to show them that not only did they not have to do pay this but I could actually save them about $36,000 of the $48,000 that they were getting ready to hand over for the previous year's return!

"You know, young man, if that were possible, our former CPA would have told us about it long ago," one of the partners retorted. I told him that his prior CPA clearly didn't know a thing about S Corporations, which led to him leaving the office a little angry. A few minutes later though, he returned.

"Wow. You're right," he replied excitedly. Yet, I could sense great anger too directed towards his now-former CPA. "He knew about S Corporations but never told us. Figured we should all pay into the system, of all things! How do we move forward, Jake?"

"The good news, Tom, is that we can do this retroactively effective for all of last year. We will be saving you many thousands of dollars on this tax bill, and for every year hereafter!"

This is the tune, my friends, that I have been singing to my clients for over 15 years. It's actually the easiest 'sell' I have ever made in my firm. So, guess what? Since you bought my book, I will share all of this with you too (as well as many more awesome tips!).

I will share not only what you can do but also the exact formula for how to do this and the detailed procedures to set this up for yourself.

The first thing you are probably thinking is likely: Don't I have to go to an attorney to do this? My answer: No, not necessarily.

Next: Is it legal to do this for last year? My answer: Yes.

Then, you'll probably wonder: How much will setting up this entity save me? My answer: I don't know but I can help you calculate it quickly.

Here's how.

Step 1 Take a look at last year's tax return. Find the profit from your partnership or sole proprietorship.

Step 2 Multiply that by 15.3 percent. This is the amount of SE (self-employment) tax you will not be paying any longer. Three important things to note.

1.   You need to pay some payroll taxes

Payroll taxes need to be paid because shareholders in S Corporations, who are active participants in the business, are required to receive wages. So, no, you don't just magically abate self-employment tax in full forever.

However, you are likely to save about one-half to two-thirds of that amount.

2. Two tax returns per year

You will need to prepare two tax returns each year, which are the 1120S corporate return and your personal 1040 tax return. (You may already be filing two returns if you are a partnership filing a 1065 return).

3. You need to maintain an active LLC at all times

With the payment of a nominal fee (usually about $75 annually), you file an annual report with the Secretary of State in order to maintain an active LLC.

That's it as far as costs go. From here, it's all saved dollars!

Here is an example to illustrate the savings you could receive:

Item	$
Net income	60,000
Self-employment tax you would owe	9,180
Gross amount saved	9,180
Payroll taxes to be paid	(3,060)
Additional fees incurred annually *	(500)
Net estimated annual savings	5,620

*Fees may include corporate taxes, payroll processing costs, corporate entity renewal fees, etc.

Only 7.7% of small businesses are doing what makes them 92% less likely to get audited

Take action now to reduce your risk of audit!

ActionTax

Some of you may have been saying to yourself, right from the beginning, "Hey Jake, I'm already an S Corporation." That is excellent. In this book, I will share with you the many ways you could be saving yourself more money than you already have been. But for the rest of you (who either have or plan to have a business someday), the question has to be: "How do I get this done?"

SETTING UP YOUR S CORPORATION

This is a detailed process. You cannot and do not want to miss a single step in the process. Follow each step to a T and you cannot go wrong. Miss a step or do one thing wrong and you're sure to have problems with the IRS (Internal Revenue Service).

I have a 17-step process for dealing with state agencies, federal agencies and others. Further, I have 12 very specific guidelines you need to follow, forever after, to protect yourself. Do you want another piece of good news? Actually, I have two pieces of good news.

First, if you are not already protecting yourself as an LLC (limited liability company), the process I share here will help you to do that. It is a wise thing for you to do for yourself and for your family.

Second, when you set this structure up, you actually reduce the risk of being audited by the IRS (and by a fair margin). Did you know that, by the numbers, an S Corporation is 1/13th as likely to get audited by the IRS as compared to a sole proprietorship or partnership? The reason for this is simple.

If the IRS audits a sole proprietorship or partnership and they are able to put back $1 of profit, they receive $0.303 of it. However, if they add $1 back to an S Corporation, they only receive $0.15 (this also depends on the tax rates for the individual, some of whom may have rates lower or higher than 15 percent).

Getting set up as an S Corporation is not necessarily the answer for everyone but for businesses that are making a profit, it may just save thousands, legally and logically. If this is something you believe would benefit you, check out this business-focused website at www.smallbizzoom.com to learn all about it. If you are already an S Corporation, read on. To be frank, there's nothing that disgusts me more than paying the IRS more than they deserve!

If all of this "number" stuff is driving you crazy, don't worry. After one more explanation that's coming up, I'll be sharing many more exciting things about being an entrepreneur and doing it successfully!

If you do not take a salary as a shareholder, and you are actively participating in your business, you dramatically increase your chance of being audited!

This is because, in 2009, the IRS made it clear that S Corporation shareholders (who are active participants in the business) are required to take a reasonable salary for their position. If they do not do so, such action will trigger an IRS audit.

Take note that although you reduce self-employment tax on the profits you earn in an S Corporation, you must still pay some self-employment tax in the form of payroll for officers. The relevant question is what constitutes a reasonable salary. I cover this topic in Chapter 3.

WHEN TO GET HELP

Ask yourself these questions.

1. Do you understand that an S Corp will save you tax dollars?

2. Are you currently an S Corporation?

3. Are you currently profitable? Is this based on last year's efforts or has it been more than 90 days that you started becoming profitable?

If you said yes to any of the questions above, you may very likely need assistance in creating an entity that is in effect retroactively. This is, however, not an easy process. There are a few options you can explore to simplify the process:

1. Visit your tax professional or attorney and get this completed;

2. Visit www.smallbizzoom.com and purchase our 17-step process to create this entity yourself;

3. Contact our firm at (253) 288-8829 so that we can assist you directly.

End of Chapter Action Items

1. **Should you incorporate as an S Corporation?**

    Let's say you are profitable as a business. Should you become an S Corporation? Do you want to save tax dollars? If you work with a CPA already and have not received any advice on this, have you now asked yourself why? Contact us today to receive a free one-hour consultation because this could be the biggest tax-saving strategy you ever use. We will review your business and personal tax situation and discuss possible strategies with you.

     Call (253) 288-8829

2. **Should you incorporate as an LLC?**

    If you are not an S Corporation, at the very least, you should be structured as an LLC. This is especially critical if you own multiple businesses or properties due to the compound effect. Contact us today for a free one-hour consultation.

     Call (253) 288-8829

3. **What if you had not filed the prior year's tax return and it was a profitable year?**

    You will want to set up a Retroactive Election as an S Corporation. You cannot do this on your own so please call us to schedule your free consultation. We'll provide you with a few good solutions.

     Call (253) 288-8829

3| "Pay your Taxes" or What?

Planning an effective salary strategy and three potential tax bombshells that you need to know

Salary structures are a critical component of a good compensation program.

bout two years after learning about the goose that lays the golden eggs (which I discussed in Chapter 2), I had an enjoyable and fun consultation with a prospective client.

He had a small business. With his 30 years in the military providing a basic yet comfortable retirement check each month, he was doing pretty well. For over an hour, he had me rolling on the floor in laughter about his military experiences. But when we started discussing his business, the humor disappeared.

"Here I am working this business day after day, year after year, and all I see is a small payroll check each month. I make less money by far than my employees. Yet, I consistently work twice the number of hours," he shared with me. Needless to say, I started by asking him if he had incorporated the business as an S Corporation. He had.

"Can I see last year's tax return and your profit and loss for this year as well?" I followed up.

He pulled them out and handed them over, shaking his head and grumbling in disgust at the results they presented.

"So, RJ (that was his name, by the way), what I see here is that you have a loss on last year's return of $6,225. And, this year, you already have a loss of over $2,000. You said though that you're making an income from the business, right?" "Yes, I get an annual salary of $40,000," RJ replied.

"Okay, so what you're telling me is that you took a salary of $40,000 last year and with this and the payment of payroll taxes on that salary, you're showing a loss on your business each year. Is that correct?" "Yes, unfortunately, it is."

"You're right, unfortunately, it is. RJ, do you realize that you have literally gifted wonderful Uncle Sam several thousand dollars and then told them "thank you" as you closed the door behind you? You are giving the IRS money they don't deserve or expect!"

AN EXAMPLE OF RJ's PROFIT AND LOSS STATEMENT FROM THE PREVIOUS YEAR	
Earnings	$150,000
Regular Expenses	$110,225
Income before Officer Salary	$39,775
Salary	$40,000
Taxes	$6,000
Net Loss	($6,225)

RJ was quite stumped. "Um, okay, explain this to me please because I don't understand what you're saying."

Does your business (no matter what type of entity it is) take advantage of the fact that the use of your home (if you do work from home) can mean a deduction each year on your tax return?

"Well, RJ, I am happy to be your new tax hero! I'm gonna save you several thousand dollars," I started out. "You are taking a salary that brings your business into a loss. This, my friend, is completely useless and nonsense! Not only are you paying Self-Employment taxes (the payroll taxes) on the loss you have but you're paying other taxes as well!" I went on to explain how much he was overpaying, which was about $4,500 in taxes. I will spare you the rest of the details but I will say this. When you set up an S Corporation, the IRS sends you a notice that states that you are 'required to take a reasonable salary'."

But what is reasonable? If you make a mistake about how this is calculated, you can bring about an audit. You don't want that. Done right, however, this could save you many thousands of dollars.

There are many good resources available for you to find out more about the topic. You can do an internet search to quickly find sources for what would be a reasonable salary by job class. You could also check out details on our website - www.smallbizzoom.com.

3 POTENTIAL TAX BOMBSHELLS

Here are three things that can potentially blow a hole in the hefty tax bill some of you may be paying.

i) The little-known Officer Pay Tax Exclusions – Officers of S Corporations are exempt from Workers Compensation, Labor and Industries in some states as well as State Employment taxes. Make sure that these are not being paid through payroll for any officer of the business.

ii) The Home Office Allocation deduction – Does your business (no matter what type of entity it is) take advantage of the fact that the use of your home (if you do work from home) can mean a deduction each year on your tax return? So many believe that this is an audit flag. However, if calculated correctly, it is not. Some 25 years ago, the IRS did, in fact, audit 2,000 businesses across many industries that had this deduction, to determine its validity as a deduction. The result: they determined it to be a legitimate deduction, plain and simple.

iii) Miles vs. Actual Expenses for vehicles – The hard fact is that many corporations and sole proprietorships do not take advantage of this. Don't be one of them. Are you aware that miles traveled on your vehicle(s) can be a legitimate expense? Or are you only taking actual deductions for the business use of your vehicle(s)? If you are not accounting for the miles traveled, you could be losing a large sum of money to the IRS. I have discovered that this is not being done in most businesses.

WHEN IS A PET TAX DEDUCTIBLE?

You would be amazed at how many people ask me, "Can I deduct my pet as an expense?" Typically, I would get a quick explanation before I could even respond that their pet costs more than their children - so naturally, it should be tax-deductible! My answer, on rare occasions, is actually, "Yes, you can!"

So when is a pet tax deductible? The answer is simple. If the pet is generating revenue for you, then it is tax-deductible. So, if Lassie can start fetching the paper for the neighbors or if your sweet little cat can start catching mice for your neighbors and you are making some income from either of these, then you're in business!

I have a number of clients who are deducting their animals as an expense. Typically, these have included farms, horse ranches, dog kennels, pet grooming services and pet shows.

There are many more of these kinds of deductions, which if implemented as applicable, can save you a lot of money in the long run. Visit www.smallbizzoom.com to begin receiving our power-packed, Money-Saving Tax Tips (a monthly email newsletter) that contains easy to implement tax strategies that will increase your cash flow.

In summary, is it possible that you are overpaying the IRS? Yes, it is. Between self-employment taxes, salaries taken and expenses taken (or not taken), there is certainly a time when a second set of eyes should be looking at your business taxes.

We have a slogan used in my CPA firm that I get to update every year. This year, it is "$42 Million in refunds and counting...." I love determining, after each year of business, just how much we have saved our clients in taxes, and adding to my slogan. This should be the kind of CPA you want working for you.

And, as promised, I am done with numbers for a while. You're soon going to learn the proven strategies that can propel your business to be the best in your industry, the most highly successful business of its kind in revenues, profits and reputation! Read on.

Ongoing tax saving strategies and access to coaching

Would you like a CPA's assistance in determining exactly what the best salary to take might be? Could you be saving thousands of dollars and creating a protective shelter against the threat of an IRS audit?

If you would like to learn more about this, sign up for my webinar series. With my assistance, you can get yourself in the best possible tax situation.

Visit www.smallbizzoom.com and sign up for the Business Success Academy. Not only will you get access to tax-saving strategies but you will also get access to business coaches who will help lead you through the process of becoming the #1 most successful business in your industry.

This webinar series includes training from the world's top experts on many of the leading business strategies in our day.

End of Chapter Action Items

1. **Work on developing an effective salary strategy**

   If you are or soon will be incorporated as an S Corporation, the salary you and any company officers take need to be reasonable but not high. Remember, you can always take draws on the profits. An effective salary strategy should be an integral part of tax planning with your CPA because this strategy could save you thousands of dollars every year. Visit www.smallbizzoom.com for resources to help with this, including getting an excellent demonstration and access to our webinar series, **Master Business Strategies.**

2. **Find out what taxes you are exempt from**

   If you have officers in a Corporation, they are exempt from Labor and Industries (also known as Workmans Compensation) and State Unemployment. Check to see that you are not paying these taxes needlessly.

3. **Keep track of your mileage**

   If you do not currently take the mileage deduction but believe that it may benefit you, start tracking your mileage. Discuss actual expenses vs mileage with your tax advisor. A great app for this is MileIQ (for Apple devices) and there are several options for many cell phone carriers. We also have a baseline formula on our website to give you a reasonable estimate each year for your miles. Check it out!

4. **Home office deduction**

   Home office deduction is huge. For many, it has simply not been taken advantage of enough. If you use your personal home and other resources for business, you need to take advantage of this write-off, no matter your entity type. Different entity types deduct it differently. Consult your tax advisor for more details.

STRATEGY #2

Work "On" It, Not Just "In" It

Develop effective systems and processes
so that the business functions and
grows beyond your involvement

4 | Everyone Needs a Coach

Doing what's needed to take things to the next level

*A business coach will help you to get unstuck
and achieve business breakthroughs.*

Y ou've now received two powerful tax tips that could forever change your tax bill. You've also received two big tips to keep you out of an audit with the IRS. Did you catch them? Awesome! I've got many more great tax tips and tricks ahead. As promised, we're not going to focus on taxes any longer. Rather, we're going to begin a journey together.

Over the next few chapters, we will clearly identify and create the foundation for turning your business into the most profitable business in your industry, exactly as mine is today. In the coming chapters, we will lead you up the path of success in your business. We will cover everything from the basics that you must have in place as well the things that propel you to business "fame". We will help you turn your success into bigger successes.

This is how you succeed on this path:

1. Read this book carefully and take detailed notes. Add your particulars (as it relates to your specific business) to these notes.

2. From there, set quarterly Business Specific Goals (we will go into more detail on this shortly) and show that you have a PHD (Pig Headed Discipline) with your business in order to implement these strategies.

3. With the help of a business coach, you will establish both short and long-term milestones. Your coach will hold you accountable, at least monthly, if not weekly, and review your progress.

4. Test and measure your success along the way. Reward yourself and all who help you to succeed.

5. Repeat this process.

Wow! This looks like a big bite to swallow, right? The good news is that you now have a coach (in the form of this book) who will help you get started. Let's talk a bit about this path.

Looking back on how your business was created, did you have a wonderful entrepreneurial burst of energy one day and just quit your day job? Did you see yourself pursuing your dreams, only to find out that you now have the worst boss ever …. yourself? These are the very circumstances I have seen played out for many business owners. They became drained of the lifeblood they once had in abundance.

The solution to this problem, though, is to be found in a great book, *The E-Myth Revisited: Why Most Small Businesses Don't Work, and What to Do About It* by Michael E Gerber. I won't go into all of the details but if you haven't read this book yet, you must put it on your required reading list. (Look for my full list of required reading in a later chapter).

> I put out the most successful advertising copy my firm has ever delivered and gained a whopping 46 new clients!

This reminds me of a story I would like to share with you. I remember the day I met with a kind, much older owner of a printing business and decided to share with him my masterpiece. I had created the best sales letter that could be written by a CPA!

This sales letter was creative, yet simple, and it was going to be mailed to 5,000 businesses. I was certain of getting hundreds of new customers and many thousands of dollars in revenue to my fairly new business. Being kind, the old print shop owner asked me if he could share my work of art with a commercial copywriter.

"Of course," I said without hesitation but to my chagrin, I soon learned how worthless my letter was and how valuable his expertise proved to be.

Had I sent my letter, many thousands of dollars would have gone down the drain. But with the help of Stephen, my new advertising guru, I put out the most successful advertising copy my firm has ever delivered and gained a whopping 46 new clients!

I learned many valuable lessons from that experience. You must surround yourself with good people. You must hire an expert to help you and you must test and measure your marketing efforts. The greatest lesson, though, would come when I reported back to the print shop owner, just how 'slammed' I was. He led me to a new friend, a business coach.

When Kevin, a business coach from ActionCoach, sat across the desk from me a week later and proceeded to sell himself to me, I wanted nothing of it though. In a prior life, I had learned my lesson all too well when it concerned consultants.

In one of my former roles, I was a Financial Controller and I saw these guys coming into this large company that I helped lead, bill us hideous fees only to then leave, promising doubled profits!

In an effort designed to get him out of my office, I agreed to sit with him for a few minutes and write a list of the many things I needed to do to work "on" my business, not just "in" my business. Kevin left, saying he would be back in a month to follow-up. I didn't believe him.

Busy as ever with new clients, a month went by and I had forgotten about our appointment. Kevin had not and it didn't take long for him to convince me that a coach could really help me start making progress in growing my business.

Let me tell you with absolute clarity that the decision I made to hire him was the single best decision I made in my business, bar none! We worked on marketing, human resources, business systems, cash flow, internal controls and interpersonal relations. Slowly, every aspect of my once tiny business began to improve. The results were phenomenal!

Let me take you back to one day in particular - March 15, 2006. This was the day less than two years from the time I began working closely with Kevin. This date also happened to be the deadline for the filing of corporate tax returns which we now had a few hundred. The problem was I was bored. I was genuinely concerned that I was missing something with such a big deadline looming, and yet, I had nothing to do.

"Jake, come over to my office if you have a minute," Kevin replied to my plea for help. I was soon sitting across the desk from him, when he started to chuckle as he said to me simply, "Jake, you have just reached Mastery Level in your business. You now have a profitable business that works without you. You have a great team, a profitable business, and efficient systems in place. Your goal has been reached!" He was right.

We had hired staff, established marketing systems, business procedures and I now had a machine of a business, wherein my job was to monitor, tweak things as needed and manage staff. What a change this was from the day I stayed the night at my office, only a year prior, just to get all of the tax work I had secured completed!

"Now Jake, don't go back to the office, bother the staff and be all concerned about what everyone is doing. Instead, it's time to start working on your vision!"

I still had a tendency to micromanage at that time. However, it didn't take much for me to release the reins under those great circumstances and dive into working on my vision. My vision, as an entrepreneur, was to own ten successful businesses - the first step was now achieved!

This is why I believe that every business owner needs a good business coach if they want to establish a profitable enterprise capable of running itself without them.

A good coach sees your blind spots and helps you overcome your weaknesses. He helps you work on whatever is lacking in the business in order that you can reach your milestones. He helps you develop SMART goals and refine those strategic objectives that get ignored so easily as you build your business.

When you meet Kevin Weir of ActionCoach, your business will take a five-year leap forward in success! You can check Kevin Weir out at www.actioncoach.com/kevinweir.

I think I know what may be going through your mind as you read this. You need services like this but should you get professional help or should you just do it yourself? I face this dilemma myself frequently and so I'd like to share an experience (a rather painful one) that may shed some light on this. I call it the Butter Story.

I was embarking on my first long bike ride in 2001. This 200-mile ride took me months to prepare for but back then, I was young. I had energy and drive. I conditioned myself for months and then one fine July morning, went to Seattle to do my event.

On arriving, I watched as many started off with their fancy, light bikes. I thought to myself, "I'm just fine with my mountain bike". Off I went, and all day long, I rode until I reached the 139-mile marker. This was in a small town where I would stay the night. I arrived late and so, I missed the dinner. To my chagrin, I had blisters all over my bottom. I was not very happy.

The next morning, though, I was up and at it again, blisters and all. I suffered the last 61 miles to the destination, Portland, where I promptly dismounted from that beastly bike. Slowly and awkwardly, I began walking around the many booths and tables at the finish line. One of the men at the booth noticed me and asked whether I was feeling okay after the ride. Embarrassingly, I explained my pain to him.

"Didn't you use the butter?" he asked. "Butter," I asked, "what do you mean, the butter?"

"Didn't you get a packet at the starting line?" he answered.

"Yes, I did. Here it is as a matter of fact," I said as I handed him the packet. He pulled a little plastic container out of the packet and then kindly explained to me what biking butter is. It lubricates your bottom so that you don't blister when you ride.

Of course, it would have to be right at the end of the bike ride that I would learn of this. You don't know what you don't know until you find out what you don't know. That day, I learned a valuable lesson 36 hours too late to save me from the pain of 16 blisters I endured on that long ride. But I am all the wiser for it now.

This is why you read good books. This may also be why, at times, you hire professionals and those who have experienced the pitfalls and overcome them. They are there to help you succeed on your first time, less the pain and suffering. So, my advice is this. As you consider various issues that come up, from time to time, ask yourself what kind of leap in time, energy (and maybe, even pain) you might want to leap past in order to achieve your objective.

End of Chapter Action Items

Sign up for our Master Business Strategies Webinar Series

When it comes to taking your business to the next level, get yourself a coach and surround yourself with successful entrepreneurs. Get insights from the most successful entrepreneurs in the world. This is the formula for massive success in your business. Visit www.smallbizzoom.com and sign up now for our Master Business Strategies Webinar Series.

2. If time or finances are not so favorable

Speak with your CPA or someone who will hold you accountable in achieving measurable results in working "on" (rather than "in") your business. You need a coach who is, ultimately, a good business-savvy person who is both reliable and knowledgeable. Learn more about finding the right CPA or business coach for you by visiting our website at www.smallbizzoom.com.

STRATEGY #3

Onward to Massive Success

Building brand awareness and
differentiation is always your job

5 | An Entrepreneur at Heart

My early start, why marketing is at the heart of a business and learning what focus means

You miss 100 percent of the shots you don't take

–Wayne Gretzky, NHL Hall of Famer

At age 13, I was a young, naïve kid looking for acceptance, wanting to feel important and starting to look at those cute girls, of course. The problem was that I wasn't accepted, I didn't feel important, and of course, I kept looking at those girls only to feel that they were out of my league.

The only thing I had going for me, at the time, was the school band which I was in. The band decided to conduct a fundraiser, selling candles, of all things. One of the boys balked at the whole idea. I was just about to put in my full support for the fundraiser when Vicki, the girl of my dreams, said that she could - and would - do it, of course.

She said that she would raise more money than any boy in the band. Pressed about it, Vicki then made a deal I have never forgotten. "If any boy beats me, the highest seller can take me to the dance next month!"

When I got home, I immediately begged my mother to buy a candle but dad, a union electrician, was unemployed at the time. Money was really tight. So, I went to six homes on our street to solicit funds and was turned down flat by all of them!

I was undeterred. A date with my dream girl was on the line and I was going to be the winner! I knocked on door after door going down one street after another. Sometimes, doors were slammed in my face immediately. At other times, they politely declined and then slammed the door.

I finally locked in my first candle sale eighteen doors later. The exhilaration was nothing that I had ever experienced before! I went to the next house and sold another. Three hours later, I ended up with four candles sold. It was only my first day!

I was awake, the next morning, at 6:00 am. It was a full eight hours before band class, where we would get an update on candle sales and I would be able to announce my master salesman results.

When class finally started, the numbers were up on the board. Being early in the alphabet, my numbers were listed further up, gaining a few "ahs" and "wows". To my shock though, Trevor, the boy who spoke to my dream girl directly, put his number up shortly after and it was a nine. The class roared with excitement!

Vicki, on the other hand, waited patiently. When the time came to announce her numbers, the class gasped as she calmly announced that she had sold ten, with a further four people who would likely buy tomorrow!

I sank down in despair. I went home that day, with my tail between my legs, having no hope in the world of ever getting a date with Vicki. Being understandably irritable, I started to grate on my siblings.

So my dad took me with him when he went to visit my grandmother at the seniors' home. On arriving, my grandmother quickly caught wind of my misery and asked me what the problem was. I told her I had tried but failed to sell some awesome candles, leaving out details as to why. She listened to the whole story and then bought five candles. That was just the beginning.

Next, she brought me to visit her neighbor (whose house is full of candles) and managed to sell six more! Then, we proceeded to a few more homes and sold even more.

My entrepreneurial spirit was alive and well! With the help of my grandmother, I was back in business and determined that Vicki would, in fact, be my date.

When I finally got to band class the next day, I was in a world I had never before lived in. With 19 candles sold, I was three ahead of everyone. Even Vicki came up to me after class. I was shaking in my tennis shoes the moment she started walking over to me until school finished an hour later. It was almost as if she was taunting the others by coming over to tell me that she looked forward to being my date if I could hold the lead. The game was on!

We ran the fundraising campaign for two weeks, and for that duration of time, I sold a couple more candles every day. I heard, through the grapevine, that the only reason Trevor had sold nine was because of his mother and aunt. So he was out. Then, to everyone's shock, a new master salesman emerged – Cory.

In the first week, Cory sold only two. But after that first weekend when he had gone to an adult event, he came in tied with me at a record 24. Then, the following Tuesday, he sold three more and took the lead.

It was a blow but I had come this far and I would not lose now. I quickly learned that my target market was senior citizens. So, I covered miles around my neighborhood in search of them. By Friday, I was back in the lead but that weekend would be the last chance for all of us.

Rumor had it that Cory was going to the same adult event that weekend and would sell hundreds more, knocking me out of a date with Vicki.

With everything on the line - my developing reputation as the best salesman ever and my date with Vicki, of course - I left school Friday on foot. It was five miles to our home and I was determined that I would sell ten candles before I walked in my front door.

Slammed door after slammed door, I worked the side streets, asking, even begging, for anyone to buy my candles. At 7:30 pm, with three candles sold, my entrepreneurial spirit began to fade. Soon, I was skipping houses, heading home, trying to convince myself that my parents were likely to be getting worried about me.

As I rounded the corner on my street, I suddenly had an idea. Why not ask my neighbor if she needed her flowerbed weeded in exchange for buying five candles? It worked. Wow!

The next day, I did the same with two others. After a few hours of work, I had sold a grand total of 38 candles! This was going to give me a decisive victory and my date with Vicki.

All-day Monday, I tried to find out how many candles Cory had sold but to no avail. When band class started, I was more nervous than I had ever been in my life! Cory looked way too proud of himself, sitting in the trumpet section.

"Okay, Jake, how many did you sell?" my band teacher asked.

"I sold 38 candles!" I responded with great pride, glancing quickly at Vicki and then Cory, who didn't appear to have heard me.

Vicki had sold just 23, so my first objective was achieved. After going through nearly everyone else in the class, Cory finally got to announce his numbers. "36 candles," he said, barely audible.

My dreams had come true! So yes, I did go to the dance with Vicki, an experience I shall never forget as a 13-year-old boy. More importantly, I realized that I could do anything if I set my mind to it and I could make good money doing it too.

That was my beginning as an entrepreneur. In high school, I would win a computer, a "state of the art" Apple II, for my efforts. I did five paper routes for a year. I also started and ran a successful lawn mowing business which I sold after four years when leaving for college. I was then self-employed once again after college ended. I am now on my sixth business. Yet, let me tell you that it has not all been a bed of roses!

90 percent of every business's success lies in marketing.

YOU WIN SOME, YOU LOSE SOME

In 2011, I was ripe for a new adventure, and after nearly a year spent searching, I acquired an existing medical spa business. We didn't start out well. I hired the wrong manager. I didn't take the reins and try to make it work until it was too late. For several months, I tried to recruit good staff, advertise and build the team back.

The manager I had hired caused a number of my staff to leave, and in leaving, they took my clientele with them. Things were just not happening as I intended. Within a year, I closed the doors to what was a very profitable business and ended up losing $334,000! Luckily, I still had my CPA firm, which was continuing to blossom but it would take some years to get over those losses.

When you go through an experience like that, you learn a lot about yourself and how to profitably run a business. Like I said earlier, the single best decision I ever made was to hire a business coach. The worst decision I ever made was to invest in a business that I did not understand, and did not actively, at least for a period of time, invest my time and talent in directly.

Being an entrepreneur is very much like riding a rollercoaster. There are ups and downs. There's the exhilaration of being on top of the world and then, there's the shock and weight of being at the bottom suddenly. Yet, the experience is worth it and I wouldn't trade it for all the employment opportunities I could have taken.

Many of you reading this are entrepreneurs, so likely, you've experienced similar highs and lows. I congratulate you on taking the leap and for sticking it out through thick and thin. Most do not appreciate nor understand the risks and challenges involved nor the ups and downs you face. The good news is there is a wealth of resources out there about every facet of running a business. In the rest of this chapter, I plan to share some of these resources and things I have learned with you.

THE HEART OF YOUR BUSINESS SUCCESS LIES IN MARKETING

90 percent of every business's success lies in marketing. The key to success is understanding the business formula to use and then, with great dedication, implementing this formula in your business.

The formula I have been taught, and which I know works is termed "The Five Ways" Principle. It is based on the premise that all businesses are driven by five key profit generation areas

- the number of leads you have;
- the conversion rate of these leads;
- the average dollar sale;
- the number of transactions sold; and
- the profit margin.

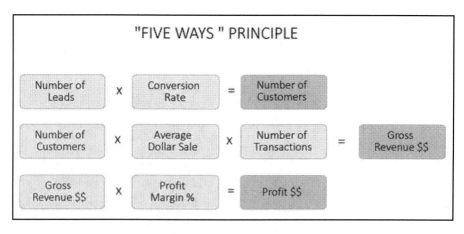

How does this formula work?

When you advertise, you create leads (the **Number of Leads**) for your business. A lead, in a marketing context, represents a potential sales contact. It could be an individual or an organization that expresses interest in either the goods or services you offer. If you do things correctly, you will be able to convert some of these leads, effectively turning interested parties into customers (the **Conversion Rate** %).

Although there are several variables, you will have a certain dollar amount of revenue generated from sales (the **Average Dollar Sale).** Provided you do right by your customer, they are likely to make more purchases in any given year (the **Number of Transactions**). The end result is gross revenue for your firm. If you spend your money wisely and can keep your overheads low (**Overhead Percentage**), this will mean you can make a decent profit.

So let's break this down with an example.

BEFORE

Let's say I spend several hundreds in advertising and produce the following results: 10 interested leads. Next, since I am effective in selling my services, I manage to close 30 percent of those leads. This means three new customers.

I sell an average of $500 to each customer and I do this five times a year. My results: 10 x 30% = 3 x $500 x 5 = $4,500 earned.

My overhead costs are set at 40 percent which makes my gross profit $1,800. Not too bad, right?

AFTER

Now, let's say I implemented the marketing strategies I mentioned (which I will cover in greater detail in Chapter 6) and increased each area by just 10 percent. What would the resulting profit be?

11 x 33% = 3.63 x $550 x 5.5 = $10,980.75 x 36% = $3,733.46!

We more than doubled the profit. By simply making a 10 percent improvement in five key areas of our business, we will now be taking home $3,733.46 rather than $1,800!

The question is: how do you achieve these results? The good news is that there are more than 300 strategies that you can choose from to increase your success in each of the Five Ways mentioned.

The implementation of these strategies, on a consistent basis, will help a business of any size increase their profits. However, it takes dedication and commitment to implement these strategies.

The most important of these strategies is Testing and Measuring Results. Test and measure the results of each of these strategies, as you implement them so that you are able to decide which to keep and which to discontinue.

Guessing doesn't work. The numbers tell a story every time and acting on the numbers is what a wise business owner does to grow consistently.

The ultimate marketing secret?

It is the CTA (Call to Action). It is an instruction to your audience to provoke an immediate response, whether that is to call you, find out more or visit your store or site.

The CTA needs to be placed on every single piece of marketing you conduct, from your advertising, in-person presentation or your business card. It needs to be everywhere!

GOAL SETTING IS CRITICAL

A great book that I was assigned to read, by Kevin my business coach, is *The Ultimate Sales Machine* by Chet Holmes. This is a must-read for small business owners in professions where selling is required.

There are very few small businesses that do not fit in that category, whether they sell as owners or hire salespeople. Many effective ideas from that book have become part of the systems I use to operate my profitable firm but there is one particular idea I would like to address here - setting and achieving your goals. Chet dedicates an entire chapter to how he succeeds in setting and achieving goals.

This is the crux of it: he identifies seven things he will do each day towards reaching his short and long term goals. I have implemented this strategy for many years and owe much of my success to this process.

Each day, I put the seven things I will accomplish that day in writing on a simple yellow sticky note and place it on my computer monitor.

The workday can get quite busy at times, I may even be in and out of the office for meetings or I could just spend most of the day completely focused on one big project. Yet, those seven items are stuck in my mind and the reticular activating system in my brain somehow, almost automatically, finds ways and means for me to complete most, if not all, of those items each day.

Consequently, I have consistently reached my quarterly and annual business objectives, year after year, and have the successful business I want.

Let's dig a little deeper here. With the help of my business coach, I have established milestones I need to hit at the quarter mark, year mark and five-year mark.

The quarterly milestones are the best, because once a quarter, I meet with my coach and dozens of my clients who are fellow business owners. We get away from work and work "on" our business. For eight hours, we focus on what we want to achieve over the next three months. The result is a precise and concise list of things we will achieve over the next 90 days. Then, each and every day, I identify seven items I will complete to support this goal.

ENTREPRENEURIAL BURST

Several times a month, I provide a free consultation session to anyone looking to start their own business. I started this in 2012 because, for several years now, business has been booming across many industries.

If you are hoping to start your own business or have been in business for less than two years, this section below is for you.

For most, the hope of starting a business is what many call an entrepreneurial burst. They have a temporary rush of entrepreneurial hopes and desires. Some act on it, dropping their JOB (what we, as self-employed individuals, define as 'Just Over Broke') and fly into the wind. They are absolutely thrilled to be their own boss and set their own hours, with big dreams of making mega-profits. This continues, sometimes, for a year and then the money begins to run low. They find themselves wearing the hat of the technician. They are the salesman, the bookkeeper, the receptionist answering every call and they have the worst boss in the world .... themselves! I recognize this because I was once here.

Now, after I began working on my business, business owners who come in to meet with me, get to reap the rewards. How? In my free consultation, I provide them with a 90-day Plan (as outlined at the end of this chapter). We carefully answer six questions relating to marketing, accounting, and business structure. The answers to these six questions help business owners focus. They provide a specific direction towards succeeding in their business. I have summarized these six concepts to help you evaluate if you are ready to take the leap.

SIX QUESTIONS ON MARKETING TO HELP YOU FOCUS

Think of the widget you're selling. It could be powerful, life-saving or perhaps, incredibly interesting and useful. Yet, if you cannot market it effectively, you can forget about any success. So, here are the six questions that can help you focus your efforts.

1) What are the 10 ways you are marketing your business?

2) What are the 10 things you are doing to close the sale with your prospective leads?

3) What are the 3 things you are doing to follow up with each lead you get? How often are you following up until they eventually do business with you?

4) What are you upselling to your existing clients?

5) What are the 3 things you are doing to increase the number of times they buy from you in a given year?

6) What are 2 things you are doing to maintain a relationship with your customers, for client retention?

No Follow Ups

No follow-up on Referrals

No capture of contact info of your leads and new customers

No follow-up of leads

No instant follow-up with new customers

No rescue of lost customers

The Complete Follow-up Strategy

Step 1
Re-state, re-sell and extend the same Offer.

Step 2
Stern/humorous "2nd Notice" tied to a hard deadline.

Step 3
"Third and Final Notice".

Step 4
Change the Offer and repeat.

This, in essence, is what the 90-day Plan focuses on. Once you have reviewed the more than 300 ways to answer these six questions, you can then drill down on a list of action items.

You then focus on 10 things you can do in the next 90 days to complete these tasks. If you can work on more than 10, that's great. There are, of course, many other aspects to running a successful business which I am not discounting here.

However, if you are able to gain predictable cash flow by marketing your services or products effectively, you solve many problems that effectively kill businesses within their first few years.

IMPLEMENT THESE STRATEGIES

At www.smallbizzoom.com, there are two ways for you to begin taking action:

1. At no cost, download a 90-day Plan, courtesy of ActionCOACH. This plan will give you a strategy, a format and many tools necessary to create a 90-day action plan to begin succeeding in your business. Included with this are more than 300 ways to market your business.

2. Join the Business Success Academy on our website. By becoming a member, you will get:

   a. one-on-one coaching by a certified ActionCoach to help you implement the strategies in this book;

   b. every resource available from the 90-day Plan above;

   c. powerful videos with insights from leading experts on business topics that include leadership, technology, marketing, tax planning and more;

   d. actionable tips on leadership and personal development, SMART goals and more;

   e. all of the resources you need, in one location, to reach your business goals.

We will give you the tools to implement the 7 Strategies in your business. Visit www.smallbizzoom.com today and start your plan to become a highly successful business owner!

5 MARKETING MISTAKES TO AVOID

1. Focus all your advertising efforts only on you and your business name.
2. Write advertisements designed to create "brand recognition". Coca-Cola can do this but you don't have multi-billion dollar ad budgets. Forget it.
3. Fail to recognize and reward those who refer business to you.
4. Allow your customers to walk out angry or unsatisfied with your service/ product.
5. Create boring, mundane or copycat advertisements.

A GIFT FOR REAL ESTATE AGENTS

Real Estate Agents present a unique category. They have distinctive ways of attracting business and are supported by an entire industry comprising powerful business coaching. Such a professional is also classified as a 1099 contractor, rather than as a business owner.

For years, we have supported Real Estate Agents by providing resources and support specifically in marketing and taxation issues. We also frequently meet with Agents at their broker and coaching meetings and provide continuing education, tax consulting and business structure advice.

We have a toolkit developed just for Real Estate Agents.

This toolkit addresses all the core topics in this book together with specific tools agents can use to drill down on simplified recordkeeping, a challenge for many busy agents.

THE TOOLKIT FOR REAL ESTATE AGENTS INCLUDES:

- tax shelters every Real Estate Agent should integrate;
- the best and latest cell phone apps for Real Estate Agents;
- systematic procedures to automate record keeping;
- entity structuring, banking and account management tips for Real Estate Agents;
- 12 Marketing Tips used by top-producing Real Estate Agents;
- tips and resources to help you become audit-proof;
- several more excellent resources.

This toolkit contains five sections of easy-to-implement business strategies that could potentially save you an average of $9,690 within the first year of implementation. Visit www.smallbizzoom.com for all the details.

POWERFUL MENTORS - 20 MUST-READ BOOKS

Succeeding in business is hard but you don't have to do it all alone. Successful leaders and business owners can guide you on this journey. Below are some of the best books to read as a business owner, whether you're new or a seasoned professional. Happy reading!

If you're new in business:

- The E-Myth Revisited by Michael E Gerber;
- The Entrepreneur Roller Coaster by Darren Hardy;
- Rich Dad, Poor Dad by Robert T Kiyosaki;
- Make Every Day Count by John C Maxwell;
- The 5 Love Languages by Gary Chapman.

If you're an active business owner:

- The 7 Habits of Highly Effective People by Steven R Covey;
- The Ultimate Sales Machine by Chet Holmes;
- The 21 Irrefutable Laws of Leadership by John C Maxwell;
- The Entire ActionCoach series by Bradley A Sugars;
- The 5 Levels of Leadership by John C Maxwell;
- Influence by Robert B Cialdini;
- The One Minute Manager by Ken Blanchard;
- Who Moved my Cheese? by Spencer Johnson;
- The Entire NO BS series by Dan S Kennedy;
- Guerrilla Marketing by Jay C Levinson;
- Marketing Professional Services by Mike Schultz;
- How to Fascinate by Sally Hogshead.

If you're a senior business owner:

- Billionaire in Training by Bradley A Sugars;
- Good To Great by James C Collins;
- Money: Master the Game by Tony Robbins.

These books are a good start. You might have noticed that I threw in a few books you may think are not related to business but they are. If you are in a relationship and running a business, *The 5 Love Languages* is a must-read. It will help you get through trying times. Many may not think of leadership books as business books but those who think that way do not understand what leadership really is.

What's coming next is the icing on the cake! We're getting into the details of what it takes to make your business the number one most successful business in your industry. So, read on.

End of Chapter Action Items

1. **Begin working 'on' your business today.**

    As we have covered in several areas of this chapter, the 90-day Plan is the key to successfully growing, systematizing and leading your business. We give you more than 300 ways to grow your business, tools to help you systematize and other resources so that your business is able to run itself without you. Enquire at www.smallbizzoom.com and you will receive detailed instructions on how to turn your business into a profitable enterprise capable of running itself without you.

2. **Bridge the knowing-doing gap**

    When reading this or any other book, do the following:

    1) Take exhaustive notes of ideas you'd like to implement as well as ideas that come as a result of reading great material;

    2) Once you've completed a book, create a list of actionable items to work on;

    3) Integrate your list into your goals and daily action items; and

    4) Celebrate every time you complete one of the actionable items!

3. **Develop this habit**

    Make it a habit, every morning, as you begin your workday, to write down seven things you will do each day. Keep this in view all day long. If you are incredibly busy working in your business each day, this becomes even more important. Your goal is to begin working 'on' your business so that eventually your business will do more work for you.

6 | Making Success Come to Life

How to begin marketing your business effectively

Marketing is no longer about the stuff that you make but about the stories you tell

–Seth Godin

ELEMENT 1: LEAD GENERATION

The very first step in generating new leads is to clearly define your target market. A target market is defined as the most precise and specific demographics and characteristics that represent your ideal client.

You can carry out the following steps to help you define your target market.

TARGET MARKET FORENSIC IDENTIFICATION PROCESS

When thinking of your target market, it's best to narrow this down to the desired persona and ask yourself these questions about them.

1. What are their purchasing habits or likes/dislikes as well as desired perceptions that attract them to you?

2. Why would they use your product/service and thus, who are they?

3. What kind of personality might they have - do they typically shop only at boutiques, are they very cautious investors, etc?

4. What detailed demographics can you pull together about them including the neighborhood they live in, places they might frequent, books they might read, activities they might indulge in, their average family size, their preferred communication methods, income level, education level, likely professions, age, sex, ethnicity and so on?

5. What groups, events or organizations might they be part of - athletics, gamers, clubs, churches, schools, professional organizations, fairs, etc?

6. Are there particular events that have occurred that may make them ideal clients? This might include the fact that they recently moved, changed jobs, were involved in an accident, had a baby, graduated, retired or even won the lottery!

This process of defining your target market helps you identify better who your potential clients are and how they live including how they spend their money. By gaining this clarity, you will then know where to look for them, what makes them tick and how you can begin attracting them.

Attracting these potential clients involves you marketing yourself to them. While there are many ways to do this, I suggest that you focus on digital marketing (as compared to traditional marketing) to do so.

Of the many benefits, these are the ones I would highlight:

1. **a leveled playing field** - armed with a solid digital marketing strategy, your business can compete with a competitor of any size;

2. **reduced cost** - a digital strategy can cost significantly less than traditional advertising channels such as the Yellow Pages, television, radio or print advertisements;

3. **clearer measurement** - you can typically see, in real-time, what's working and what's not, which enables you to tweak your efforts during a campaign;

4. **results in real-time** - unlike traditional marketing which can take time to generate results, digital efforts can yield results almost immediately;

5. **wider reach** - print is limited to the geographical reach you can afford. Digital marketing efforts are, in essence, limitless, ensuring a long term return for fairly low upfront costs;

> Of all of the areas that make up the Five Ways Principle, it is the Conversion Rate strategy that is the least costly yet most impactful.

6. **viral capability** - traditional channels rarely afford this. Digital efforts, however, can not only ensure your message is shared but is shared repeatedly and across wider and bigger audiences than you intended, with no limitation on time. A phenomenal offer or piece of content has the ability to go 'viral', literally surpassing any expectations you may have about what is possible.

11 WAYS TO USE DIGITAL MARKETING TO CLOSE BUSINESS

There are over 75 ways to market your company. This list represents a fraction of the number of methods to do so online.

1. Employ an SEO (Search Engine Optimization) Expert;

2. Create several landing pages for your products;

3. Purchase digital advertising to draw people to your online media;

4. Create a dynamic, SEO-optimized, interactive website with compelling content that people will want to share;

5. Create compelling content email newsletters for your customers, prospects and target markets;

6. Invite website visitors to opt-in to your email newsletter and download your white papers or tips. Invite them to schedule obligation-free appointments with you or to purchase your products;

7. Find websites where you can list your business or products for free, including search engines such as Google, Bing or Yahoo. Consider also various industry-specific websites that offer business listing services for free;

8. Employ a marketing services company to do a free website assessment or review for you;

9. Create dynamic content-driven company pages on various social media such as Facebook, Twitter, YouTube, LinkedIn, Instagram, Pinterest and other social media sites you believe are appropriate for your industry;

10. Create and maintain a blog that sells your products, employs 'Calls to Action' as well as captures leads and referrals;

11. Create a system you can manage to ensure your online content is regularly and continuously updated.

DIRECT RESPONSE MARKETING

Direct Response Marketing is a type of marketing that seeks to elicit a specific response to a marketer. Typically, it facilitates the delivery of a call to action and an outcome through direct or online interaction for immediate feedback.

If you decide to use this form of marketing, you need to have a Master Plan for generating new business. The plan below is our Master Plan.

Direct Response Marketing Master Plan

Lead Generation Magnets	Compelling Website	The Main Sales Letter
Examples books, reports, CDs, online videos, Google ads, Facebook ads or anything that offers useful information of prime interest to your target market. When delivered, it establishes your authority, expertise and credibility. It also promotes your products or service. A lead is then drawn to your website to receive the information.	Your website is a digital representation of your brand, enabling you to present information about your service /products and capture the attention of those who may be interested in such a service/product. Your website is able to capture the contact information of your visitors.	The main sales letter sells your core service/ product or promotes your event etc.

The Follow-up System	Inbound Call Script
This represents an automated series of steps for converting leads that include both online and offline steps in a specific sequence. You need to read *The Ultimate Sales Machine* by Chet Holmes to create the perfect follow-up system.	This represents a consistent way for your staff to deal with inbound calls that include the capture of the prospect's contact details (so they can be followed up with) and the lead source (so you can measure which channels are producing better results).

Lead generation is the most costly part of generating revenue. The solution to addressing this high cost is, therefore, to spend more effort on converting the sale. Let's now look at several ways to convert prospective customers into paying customers.

"The most effective and least expensive way to generate leads is to offer prospects something they want and make it easy and non-threatening for them to get it."

–Dan S Kennedy

ELEMENT 2: THE CONVERSION PROCESS

I remember my first Quarterly Planning day with my business coach. He began by educating my team on the Five Ways chart. He then asked us to identify our numbers, including what percentage of leads we turned into customers.

Initially, I thought I was closing between 75- 90 percent of all business coming in. I thought I was good at selling the services that I believed in.

If only that were true.

After diligently testing and measuring the activities, I got an accurate number of how many paying customers we actually acquired.

The numbers were quite embarrassing.

I was converting about 23 percent! This, of course, provided much room for improvement.

With the help of my coach, I began to actively work on the systems and procedures that would help my staff and I increase our conversion rate.

Here are a handful of ways to increase your Conversion Rate:

1. Providing a written Guarantee;

2. Mapping your Sales Process;

3. Measuring your Conversion Rate;

4. Qualifying your leads as early as possible;

5. Creating a Benefits List which serves to focus on how the customer gains from your service/product (as opposed to advertisements which are feature-driven);

6.   Providing useful and detailed information such as brochures, diagrams, etc;

7.   Using a defined Sales Process;

8.   Preparing a Quote or Proposal;

9.   Educating the Buyer;

10. Creating Irresistible Offers.

As you can see, many of these Conversion Rate Strategies are low or no cost to create and use. It is really about developing these strategies, and then with discipline and training, integrating them into your sales process. Of all of the areas that make up the Five Ways Principle, it is the Conversion Rate strategy that is the least costly yet the most impactful.

ELEMENT 3: INCREASE THE AVERAGE DOLLAR SALE

The Average Dollar Sale represents the amount of revenue you can generate from each sale. Fast food restaurants, in recent years, have capitalized on one Average Dollar Sales Strategy that has produced greater profits for them than any other strategy. This, in two words, is "Super Size". Look at the list below and consider what things you might do to increase your Average Dollar Sale.

1.   Increase your Prices;

2.   Change your Product or Service Mix;

3.   Bundle your Offerings;

4.   Add-on Sales;

5.   Train your sales force to make the higher dollar sale.

Increasing your price is the easiest and simplest way to increase revenues. If you are concerned that doing this may result in a loss of clients, there are a few steps you can take to minimize this:

1. Add greater value to support your increased prices;

2. Talk up the benefits and value of your product; and

3. When faced with some resistance to the price, provide tiered pricing options or discounts.

Just do it anyway. A 5 percent increase in your price has the power of generating a 14 percent difference to your profit. At the same time, the likelihood of losing your customers is less than 1 percent. The bottom line - the increased profits are staggering in impact.

In my third year of business, my coach suggested I raise my prices. At first, I was quite apprehensive and concerned. I didn't want to get a bad reputation or lose customers. My coach worked on me for months, and with great fear, I decided to increase my rates. Results: zero loss in customers and a 26 percent increase in my company's profits.

ELEMENT 4: INCREASE THE NUMBER OF TRANSACTIONS

In some industries, the number of transactions that can be generated per customer is fixed. For example, a tax return is generally prepared only once a year. Other industries may be highly leveraged and therefore, more profitable because they can sell products multiple times.

Take a restaurant business where meals can be provided three times a day, seven days a week potentially. With this in mind, here are a few ways you can increase the number of transactions with each of your customers:

1. Sell memberships;

2. Offer coupons for future business;

3. Have an nth service/sale for a free offer;

4. Follow Up and Upsell; and

5. Offer exclusivity and/or specials to specific target audiences.

ELEMENT 5: INCREASING PROFIT MARGINS

So, let's summarize the formula briefly. First, you get leads by advertising. Second, based upon what you do with these leads, you convert a certain percentage of them into paying customers.

The product of leads multiplied by the conversion rate gives you the number of new customers. Then, using successful selling strategies and techniques, you increase the average dollar amount of each sale transacted. By building relationships and following systematic procedures, you increase the number of times customers buy from you (number of transactions).

> No. of Customers x Average $$ Sale x No. of Transactions
> = Gross Revenue

By implementing the strategies I've provided, along with over 300 more available in our 90-day Plan (get this on our website), you can begin making micro improvements in each section of your marketing.

FIVE KEYS TO CLOSING THE SALE

1. Get your customer to say "Yes" at least five times.
2. Imply your customer's acceptance and desire to act or make a purchase.
3. Always, always, always ask for the sale.
4. Make sure that you've got a visible, clear Call To Action every time.
5. Create and implement a 10-step follow-up process.

End of Chapter Action Items

1. **Create a SMART Goals List**

    Do some internet-based research on your industry and on the strategies mentioned here. Get more details about the newest and best ways to improve your marketing efforts.

    Then create a SMART Goals list so you can begin integrating these activities into your business today. Once you see our full list of over 300 marketing tools, incorporate this into your ongoing daily goals and 90-day plan. Go to www.smallbizzoom.com to get the 90-day Plan.

2. **Consider new revenue streams you can create from existing clients**

    Review your list of customers and your business structure. What additional products, services or intangibles could you be upselling to your clients? Take this seriously. This is a precious list of people who know and trust you. In my landscaping business, I was upselling fertilizing, window cleaning, gardening, landscaping, pruning, pressure washing, gutter cleaning, thatching, aerating, moss removal, clean-up projects and more. I eventually added painting and other contracting services which I then sold to other businesses.

    Could you be providing insurance for what you do, a warranty or a service contract? How about dessert, a soft drink or a full meal deal – supersized?

    What complementary new products or services could supplement your current products? Make a list and take action to test whether you could develop a few viable and new revenue streams.

7 | Connect Powerfully

Why my epilepsy has been a critical factor in my client retention strategy

Trusting our intuition often saves us from disaster

–Anne Wilson Schaef

When I was a month old, I was rushed to the hospital after suffering a horrible convulsive seizure. My parents soon learned that I had Spinal Meningococcal Meningitis. I survived but my parents were warned that I could suffer serious side effects.

Around the time I turned eight, I began to suffer mild seizures during the daytime. Over the years, these then grew into what are called complex partial seizures (seizures that cause you to become unconscious and they affect a part of your brain). My memory began to suffer. However, by the time I became a teenager, my entrepreneurial spirit overcame any limitations caused by these seizures.

At 17, I was finally diagnosed with epilepsy and put on medication. For years, I would change medication many times as my body quickly developed a tolerance to the drugs and as the seizures grew in intensity. Getting through college was especially hard as the seizures began to impact my ability to memorize and focus, which was critical in preparing for the CPA exam.

At 40, I had the memory of a 90-year-old. I knew something had to give. So, after 23 years with the same neurologist, I decided to get a second opinion. Unbeknownst to me, I selected one of the best in the state. I learned that surgery was an option. I immediately begin pre-surgery work to determine whether surgery was going to be possible.

It was around this time that I had a new potential client visit my office. Usually, I never discuss my epilepsy with my clients, and certainly, not with new potential clients. Yet, for some inexplicable reason, I began sharing details of my medical situation with him. We talked for about half an hour, after which he suggested I visit the Burrow Institute in Arizona to get at least a consultation because epilepsy was one area they specialized in.

He insisted I write down the details of the doctor's name and address etc after which I then asked him why he was seeing me. He replied that he had an estate tax return to prepare and would come to see me when it was ready. Rather abruptly, he stood up, thanked me and said goodbye, reminding me that he would return when he was ready to file that estate tax return. I immediately thought, "I will never share my epilepsy again with a potential client." I felt he would likely not return and that I had scared him away.

I'll move through this story quickly now. I soon learned I could have surgery and met with the first neurosurgeon. His suggestion was to remove a big segment of my brain that oddly was not even directly impacted by the cause of my epilepsy (the meningitis I had suffered had destroyed one small part of my brain).

He also told me I needed to seriously consider the side effects as I could lose my career with this kind of surgery and the costs would top half a million too. My wife and I left distraught and crushed.

While at the office, the next day, I began to recollect (remember, I had a very bad memory) my meeting with that potential client who suggested I contact a particular hospital. Slowly and with effort, I remembered that I had written a note about it and then locating that note, I called the hospital and scheduled a consultation. It was the middle of tax season, I would need to fly to Arizona, and in many ways, I almost chose not to pursue this.

> People do business with those they *know and trust*.
> Period.

After this, I then went for my second consultation, which was already scheduled for, in Seattle. At this point, I had done my homework and I had many questions for these two neurosurgeons, who suggested a much more precise method of removing just the damaged part of my brain. They then suggested I consider gamma-knife radiation. They were in the fifth and final stage of a study on this procedure, and because I met all 17 requirements, I was a candidate for a free procedure! Accountants like free stuff. It was great to hear of a new, much better option that was non-invasive and took only two hours.

I was convinced to move forward but my wonderful, cautious wife was not. She felt I needed to wait a few months and then fly to Arizona for another consultation. I thought it was a bad move to spend all this money, waste more time and endure more seizures when this new procedure was clearly the newest and greatest thing for me to explore.

Yet, over the weekend, my wife won. In the end, I waited a few more months and endured many more seizures until March 2012 when I left for Arizona to meet Dr. Smith at the Burrow Institute.

I asked him for his opinion on the options I was considering in Washington state and within two minutes, he had thrown out the first option, asking me why that first doctor was suggesting a 40-year-old procedure. He had trained the doctors who were providing the second option. Then I told him about the gamma-knife procedure.

"I am head of radiology here and have done gamma-knife more than 3,000 times. I will not do it for you," he said immediately. "Oh okay, why?," I asked in shock. "Come to my private office and I will show you why." He then showed us two pictures on his computer.

The first was a picture of a person's brain with cancer.

"Now this person needed and did undergo gamma-knife in Washington DC because the cancer was too deep for conventional surgery." Then he showed us the second picture.

"But this is the result of it." The second picture showed massive brain swelling where the gamma-knife was performed.

"As is so often the case, this is the danger of gamma-knife. This man is in surgery prep now and I will soon perform a procedure to, hopefully, save his life, as he has been sent to me. You, however, don't need to take these risks, and so, I will not do this procedure for you."

"Wow! So, what do you suggest, Dr. Smith?," I asked, realizing quickly that I was speaking with an exceptional and renowned expert.

"We will come in under the side of the brain, and using ultrasound, remove that one tiny spot in the brain and touch nothing else in the brain that is healthy." It was that simple.

As we drove back to the airport that day, I began to wonder about all that I had heard and learned about. Then, it dawned on me - who was the man who came into my office and told me about this doctor?

His insistence on my taking down all those details ensured that I was where I am now - with a far better surgical option. I went through the procedure which was completed flawlessly and my epilepsy was cured. The only side effect is, as Dr. Smith pointed out when I asked about side effects, "an end to your epilepsy."

My wife began to tell everyone we knew about the "angel" who came to her husband's office. For some time, I tolerated her "sharing the story" in that manner. Then one day, it dawned on me that I had a digital calendar system of all my appointments. I could actually find out who this guy was. I would call him, thank him and give him a free tax return as a thank you.

Yet, the strange thing is that I will never find out. Despite looking through every day in September 2011, the month he visited me, I found nothing. Even reviewing the three months before and the three months after the date I knew he had come by, I found nothing.

I asked my receptionist if she ever deleted appointments that took place and got an odd, "No, why would I? It's in the past and good for a reference anyway."

I will never know who came to my office that day but I do know this. Firstly, I am being watched over and this was an answer to many years of prayers. Secondly, even among experts, there are those who know their stuff better than others. Finally, always take the time to get a second or third opinion even when you think you have the best doctors in the state!

So, why have I shared this lengthy story here? I have many reasons, but more importantly, the question is who do I share this story with? Well, I share it with every client I have. Why?

It has been the number one way I have increased client trust, and then referrals, and ultimately, client retention. LCV refers to lifetime customer value. People do business with those they *know and trust.* Period.

This story often creates shared interests and concerns with my client. In my being authentic and more personal with them, these clients then open up, creating real connections that can last far beyond customer concerns that might arise in the future.

CREATING AUTHENTIC CONNECTIONS

Client retention is created one client at a time by being authentic, sharing inspiring stories, providing stellar service (almost as if you treated them as your family) and having authentic connections.

There are many touchpoints or shared experiences for authentic connection with the people you do business with including:

- the fact that they may have children;
- they may have a love for certain places like Disneyland, for example, or certain activities like hiking;
- they may have only boys or girls in their family; or
- they may have similar hobbies, interests, political views, religious views or have the same ethnic background.

I never communicate with my clients only about my products, services and business. I don't want them to just be customers. I ask about their business and family and then, with that, I usually find some common ground. Often, our conversations are on interesting topics, making whatever I sell much easier because there is a level of trust involved.

When you've given your client a great experience, it is easy to ask for referrals and the best time to ask is when they love you the most. Typically, you'll know when based on the feedback you get when providing great customer service. Here is a method I use to ask for the referral.

ONE POWERFUL REFERRAL METHOD

When a client expresses that they are happy with my service, I pull out three business cards. On the first card, I write my cell phone number. I tell them specifically that I do not give this number out to everyone but that I want to make sure that their every need is met. Therefore, if they have any questions, they can call me personally.

Next, I hand them two more business cards, the backs of which have space for them to write down the name, email and phone number of a referral. I ask them to think of two individuals they know who would benefit from my service as they have. I then tell them I will get a drink and be back shortly. When I return, I usually see the cards have been filled in. If the cards are still not filled in, I sit down and remain silent. Usually, I will see at least one, often two names, written down. I go on to ask them pertinent questions about these prospects, beginning a process of qualification.

I ask if they would prefer me calling them first or the prospect. I confirm that I can use their names when I call these prospects. In effect, I ask enough questions so that when I call these prospects, I can ask appropriate questions using their name, can refer to their business name and maybe even discuss a tax concern they may be having. Finally, I call the prospect, either with my client present or not, and introduce myself. I invite them to lunch or a consultation, whichever seems appropriate. I am careful to follow this process, step by step.

I implement a similar follow-up process with referrals I receive through email and through our CRM system which draws many referrals from our new and existing clients. I also have a written process that my receptionist uses for doing the same thing during our busy tax season.

We receive hundreds of referrals every year but only 30 percent are actually interested and ready to switch CPAs. With that in mind, we keep track of these people in our referral campaign system in my CRM software. By doing so, we ensure that our firm is front of mind when it is time for them to make a switch. Until such time, we dazzle them with resources offered and special offers. It works, and works well!

Here are a few other referral methods you can use:

1. Send your family or friends to us and we'll give you $25 in cash;

2. When you give us a referral, we will send you $20 in $2 bills;

3. Send us a referral as part of X competition and win a brand new iPad, a trip to Las Vegas with all the perks and many more;

4. Every referral you give us earns the Charity of Your Choice $25, $100 or more;

5. Ask, then Follow Up and Reward the giver and new customer.

IMPLEMENT A REFERRAL CAMPAIGN

Our firm has created and implemented new referral campaigns nearly every year. We have given cash for a single referral, compounding cash for multiple referrals as well as prizes and gifts to both referrers and those being referred. We have asked for referrals through special letters, directly in person, during special appreciation events, whenever they appear awestruck with our service and many more.

Here are 11 things that you should work on creating an impression so that clients know there is an active Referral Culture in your business:

1. Our customers provide referrals.

2. Our good customers refer often.

3. Our best customers refer often.

4. We generally expect you to provide a referral.

5. Referrals are genuinely appreciated.

6. Referrals are well taken care of.

7. Not referring someone is weird and inappropriate. You should feel bad about it.

8. Here are many reasons people do business with us [state these reasons clearly].

9. Most people are not able to find a good, trustworthy provider of these services. Therefore, you are doing them a great service by telling them about us.

10. There are easy ways to introduce us to others and here is some information for you to do this [provide this information].

11. So, here's how you can refer someone [provide the exact steps of what needs to be done].

As a final note on referrals, you may squirm when I tell you how I have given as much as $200 away for a referral. The reality is that you are "giving" at least the cost of acquiring a client if you bought an advertisement.

So, if you calculated that amount and gave that money instead to the individual who is referring a customer (these customers will usually have some loyalty built-in), then you would be winning big!

THE VALUE OF RETENTION

A US News and World Report study determined that the average US-owned business loses 15 percent of its customers each year, in one of the following ways:

- 68 percent leave due to their feeling a lack of, poor or indifferent service;
- 14 percent leave due to unresolved disputes and complaints;
- 9 percent leave because of price;
- 5 percent are drawn away by a recommendation for your competitor; and
- 1 percent die.

This means that 82 percent of customers leave due to a customer service issue. This is an area where you can have a direct impact on your customer losses. Yet, many business owners do nothing, make no financial investment in regaining these lost customers who they may have paid hundreds of dollars per customer to acquire!

If you are serious about getting referrals from your current clients, you need to be serious about customer service. What is the potential lifetime value of a client in your industry? If you spend the money to retain these clients and solve their problems, is it worth it?

Let's look at the numbers below, for a successful client of mine (who is in the food and beverage line) and the formula for Lifetime Customer Value.

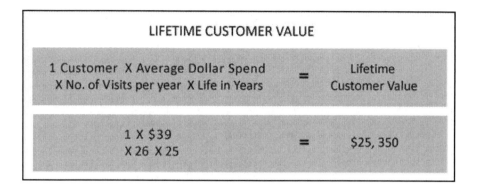

LIFETIME CUSTOMER VALUE

1 Customer X Average Dollar Spend X No. of Visits per year X Life in Years	=	Lifetime Customer Value
1 X $39 X 26 X 25	=	$25, 350

1. We determined that his regular customers come in, on average, once every two weeks and they spend $39.00.

2. One industry standard puts the life of a restaurant customer at 25 years. We determined that, if any of his loyal customers did not return after three weeks, he ought to be reaching out to them and offering them something to return.

3. After dividing his annual advertising costs by the number of new customers he acquired, we found that the cost of getting a new customer was $176.

4. We learned two things:

   a) if a customer was unsatisfied, providing a free meal was far less than the cost of acquiring a new customer; and

   b) a simple offer to bring the existing customer back, like providing a $25 off coupon, would likely save our client $150 or more, as his acquisition cost for a replacement customer was $176.

When you consider the added value of a happy client who gives referrals, comes by often, spends money repeatedly on you, brings his friends and family to do business with you, you then realize that the real value of a satisfied, long-term client can easily be over $100,000. What are you doing to retain and keep your clients happy?

14 WAYS TO RETAIN YOUR CLIENTS

1. Ensure that every interaction with them includes a show of gratitude for their business.

2. The number one desire of human beings is to be admired. Figure out how to show admiration for your clients.

3. Show some form of customer appreciation for your clients in any direct way you can. This could be by holding an event, sending thank you, birthday, anniversary or Christmas cards, making a personal call to them or conducting a satisfaction follow-up questionnaire, etc.

4. Initiate a formal Rewards Program that could include rewards for doing additional business with you, providing you with referrals, being a returning client for a year, two years or a decade, etc.

5. Ensure that every employee of yours is a Customer Service Diplomat.

6. Implement a specific and consistent process for how complaints are resolved with urgency.

7. Send out email and/or print newsletters that are packed with compelling content.

8. Throw a grand appreciation party periodically.

9. Do something special for the Top 5 percent of your customers each year.

10. Perform customer service training for your staff consistently, being clear about your expectations.

11. Develop marketing paraphernalia like mugs, pens or other items, with either your name or theirs on them and send them out to your clients.

12. Provide memorable gifts for clients for referrals given, for the number of years they have stayed as a client or for specific purchases they have made.

13. Produce and send out Special Reports, white papers, educational information or any other good content on subjects of mutual interest between you and your clients.

14. Follow up courteously, diligently and effectively with every new person who is sent your way.

A great book that provides some quick reading on this is The Happy Customer Handbook by Keith Lee. I highly recommend reading this book and taking notes so that you can start implementing the ideas immediately because they are easy to do.

One of the best ways I know to increase client retention, whatever your business may be, is to create a membership program. In such a program, you create different levels of membership. This may range from free right up to a premium level where there are exclusive offers available for purchase.

On a final note, you might have noticed that sometimes I talk about the customer while at other times, I refer to the client. A client tends to be one to whom you provide services to whereas a customer tends to be a buyer of your product. While they are often used interchangeably, it is good to take note of this subtle distinction because treating someone as a customer may imply a short-term relationship whereas clients are typically viewed as long-term relationships. Consequently, the manner in which you view the relationship - actual and potential - will have some bearing on how you treat them.

The Business Success Academy

Some who read this book will dig into it and use it to fill every hole in their business. Others need a program, an organized system to follow.

We all need good leaders and experts to help us reach the pinnacle of success in our business. To this end, we have created a webinar series called The Business Success Academy, exclusively for you and your business, to help you achieve massive success.

The Business Success Academy includes six months of personalized, business-focused webinars, one-on-one coaching from a certified ActionCOACH and training provided directly from some of the world's leading entrepreneurs who want you to succeed. Everyone who signs up for the Academy becomes a member for life, thus giving them access to a lifetime of resources that will help them succeed.

Organize your strategies for success. Take a five-year leap forward in business success. Get the best insights from business coaches and many highly successful entrepreneurs. Visit www.smallbizzoom.com today to sign up.

You've created your business path. Now let's turn it into the most successful business in your industry.

End of Chapter Action Items

1. **Make a difference**

   If you know anyone who is suffering from epilepsy and is not seizure-free, have them look into the Burrow Institute in Phoenix, Arizona.

2. **Create relationships of trust**

   Find as many ways as you can to open the doors of communication with your clients so that you create trust with them right from your first meeting.

3. **Start asking for referrals**

   Whether you decide to use my methods or some other methods, ask for referrals. What's important is to start. Begin when clients show you they are satisfied with your work. Establish a method for getting referrals for you and your employees. Reward those who give referrals. The more you reward them, the more they will give.

4. **Read this book**

   The *No BS Guide to Maximum Referrals* by Dan Kennedy. I got better ideas, on how to get massive referrals from my clients, from this book than any other.

5. **Re-work your business card so it is more effective**

   i) Ensure there is a place on your card for you to ask for a referral and for them to write that referral down;

   ii) Provide a compelling call to action that provides them an immediate benefit if they take action;

   iii) List the benefits of providing referrals - these should not all be about you or your business;

   iv) Create lead magnets online so people are drawn to you and you have the opportunity to capture their information so you can market your services to them;

v) Do not go cheap on your business card. Pay attention to your choice of colors, the finish, the size of the card and your design so that you get people taking a second look. They could very well be your next big customer.

6. **Sign up for our Master Business Strategies Webinar series**

Visit www.smallbizzoom.com to sign up today. Take the next step toward becoming the most successful business owner in your industry.

STRATEGY #4

Master the Money Game

Develop new revenue streams and understand cash flow better

8 | Money is Meant to be Compounded

Potential revenue streams, planning for retirement and choosing the right advisor

*#1 Make money. #2 Use that money
to make more money. #3 Repeat*

–Anonymous

At age 15, I bought my own lawnmower. Previous to this, the five paper routes I ran were giving me about $550 a month. It was a great income for a 14-year-old but I did not feel the same when I turned 15!

THE SEED OF ENTREPRENEURSHIP

Lying in bed one night, unable to sleep, as usual, I began contemplating ways to make money from all of my customers. At first, I thought I would sell them my own paper (I was 15 - I could conquer the world!) but luckily, I soon dispensed with that idea. At some point that night, I stumbled on the idea of mowing lawns.

Twelve hours later, I had my first customer, a paper route customer right behind my house. At that point, I did not have a lawnmower. It took just a week to collect enough paper route profits to buy a used lawnmower, weed killer and gas can. It was a lot of work, a ton of fun and a teenager's dream.

Within a few months, I had 40 lawn customers. I then quickly realized that there was little money in paper routes but excellent money at $15 - $20 apiece, mowing lawns once a week.

By the end of the summer, I was ready to purchase my first car. It was an El Camino and I was thrilled! The exhilaration was akin to taking a ride on a roller coaster, but as you know, what goes up must come back down. That it did with the rainy weather in the fall. I found myself suddenly in debt to several people for equipment, burdened by credit card debt and a cash loan.

I had no way to make the money I needed. I don't remember the exact amount but it must have been around $1,500 which, at the time, could make any teenager genuinely worried.

My dad listened to me worry and beg for help, again and again, but to my shock, he would not (maybe, even could not) help me financially. In hindsight, it was the wisest thing he ever did for me.

It was excruciatingly painful to look at that piece of paper recording all the money I needed. In the back of my mind, I feared I would have to sell my cherished car but I was determined there had to be another solution. It was snowing though. So, how would I mow, fertilize or even prune? Ah… I could shovel snow. I had 40 customers. Off I went for the rest of the winter vacation, day after day. On the day I returned to school, I broke even.

> Looking back at my experiences holding down jobs and my own entrepreneurial activities, I learned one overarching rule about money. The name of the game is cash flow.

When spring came, and I had a car to work with, a newspaper to give me customers, and ambition overflowing, I realized the value of hiring a good worker. I went through about ten workers before I found a good one and when I did, the profits began to increase. I started to add many more services to my "Services List".

At 16, I was learning quickly the benefits of the upsell, which for me at the time, included clean-up projects, fertilizing lawns, window cleaning, moss removal, thatching, pruning, roof cleaning - the list goes on and on.

During my senior year, I was "Jake the Snake, Gardeners," a nickname one of the popular kids at school called me once that stuck. I was the richest kid in high school, making about $30,000 annually.

THE START OF MY LOVE AFFAIR WITH ACCOUNTING

During the winters of those school years, I had to get a job and I found it hard to work for anyone else, especially for that measly minimum wage of $4.35. Job after job, I just could not find any satisfaction. I was an entrepreneur back then, even if I didn't know it and looking back, I know now why I could never hold a job for long.

Every winter was a struggle while the rest of the year was fabulous. I needed a solution and I found it in going to college to learn business management. This quickly morphed into Accounting because I had a great love for numbers.

I graduated from college with a job offer of $42,000 annually. I struggled with jobs though, and over a ten year period, I went through a whopping 23 employers. It was not about the money but I knew something had to change. It was then that I decided to break away and start my own accounting firm. That, my friends, was the golden ticket.

Looking back at my experiences holding down jobs and my own entrepreneurial activities, I learned one overarching rule about money. The name of the game is cash flow.

Cash flow is king. There were many times I struggled as I moved between jobs. Conversely, when I found my niche and began filling a need, whether that was in lawn mowing or professional accounting services, I made a killing when my passion and skills met another's needs.

One of the things I enjoy greatly today is being able to share this story with the men and women who come in for advice on starting their own business. I have developed excellent resources that help those who are starting their businesses. These complement the other resources I have built as a result of my working with a business coach. Feel free to check out my firm's website, www.actiontaxteam.com because almost every page on the site contains forms, tools and tips to help the small business owner. This includes services on marketing, bookkeeping, taxes, entity structure, education on QuickBooks software and much more.

MASTERING THE INVESTING GAME

If you do get involved in any kind of investing activity, either within a 401K or other pre-tax instrument, you will be intimately aware of the ups and downs associated with the market.

The goal of investing, many would concur, is to follow a general, long term upward trend in the stock market. You would move along with the highs and lows of the market in the short term but ultimately, you are looking for earnings from the long term growth of your investments. It is, therefore, rather unfortunate for those who do this to then discover that they are only earning about two-thirds of their actual portfolio growth. The rest of the money is being earned but not by them.

Who is earning the rest of it? It is the financial advisor, and all of the behind-the-scenes money managers, who earn this in the form of fees and commissions. Many are simply unaware of how much of the income and profits within their portfolio are eaten up by these different advisors. They use the best tools possible to hide the commissions and administrative fees they charge.

Let me illustrate this point. Let's say that, of late, your portfolio has been earning a reasonable 8 percent return on your investment. This figure, however, is not the actual rate of return you are earning. More likely, your investment is earning close to 12 percent or more. What happens is your earnings will drop by about 4 percent through the year due to all the commissions and transaction fees.

What does this mean in terms of lost dollars, compounded over many years of growth? Well, in the first year, the cost is as much as $4,000 for every $100,000 in your portfolio. Compounded over many years, it can easily break a million dollars in lost retirement!

Have you wondered how much your 401K plan administrator fees are costing you? While it is a complicated process to find out the specific forms necessary to determine the fees, the good news is that it is easy to find out exactly how much you could be overpaying. Simply go to http://americasbest401k.com/fee-checker/ for them to conduct an independent evaluation of your fees instantly.

This site, besides helping you determine your fees, also has the best overall 401K option that I have found in the United States. They have a flat fee of .075 percent as compared to the average 4 percent. This is really the best available in the US today as far as I am aware and this is one of the most powerful ways to begin mastering the game of money, from an investing perspective.

GETTING THE LOWDOWN ON YOUR BASELINE RETIREMENT NEEDS

I am regularly asked by my clients to help them determine how much money they need to retire, both the minimum and a comfortable amount. There are many variables at play from your age, income level, retirement plans as well as savings levels.

So I always suggest they go see a qualified financial advisor. But then I go on to share with my clients my down and dirty calculations for determining their baseline retirement needs.

First, we take a quick look at their monthly cash requirement today. We calculate some estimates as to what this will look like at the age they retire.

Once we have a reasonable calculation for their cash outflows, we look at their existing income streams on retirement, including social security, pensions, 401K distributions and even such things as a possible reverse mortgage or sale of assets. Look at the example below.

The Johnson Family	
Monthly Cash Outflows	
Mortgage (Loan, Insurance, Property Taxes)	$1,200
Other debt (Auto loans, credit cards, etc)	$200
Utilities (Electric, Internet, Cable, Gas, etc)	$400
Auto (Vehicle loan, gas, repairs & maintenance)	$400
Insurances (Auto, home, life, etc)	$600
Food, Clothing, etc	$300
Medical Expenses	$700
Other	$200
Fun Money	$300
Total Monthly Requirement	**$4,000**

The Johnson Family	
Monthly Cash Inflows	
Social Security	$1,300
Pension	$1,500
Monthly Demand from Investments	**$1,200**
Total Cash Inflows	**$4,000**

The question, in this scenario, is: How much money will they need to have in retirement (whether in cash reserves or available saleable assets) in order to live comfortably? The average lifespan today, after retirement, at 65 years of age is about 30 years between two people.

Monthly Demand $1,200 X 30 years = $432,000.

Simplifying the many calculations involved and leaving out many variables, you can see that they would need approximately $432,000 saved by the time they retire if they wish to live semi-comfortably.

You can do the same simple calculation for yourself. There is a great tool on my website at www.smallbizzoom.com which you can use. This tool contains a few more ways for you to get a closer estimate but, once again, this is a gut check. My suggestion is for you to see a good investment advisor so you can make some good choices about saving towards your retirement. This brings me to my next topic: Who qualifies as the right kind of investment advisor?

CHOOSING THE RIGHT INVESTMENT ADVISOR

There are two kinds of investment advisor. The first, which is more common, is the kind who works for the local, big chain firm. He is very effective at getting you to sign up for all the funds that will get him the highest commissions and he will most likely get you into mutual funds which lose money most of the time.

When you add to this, some risk assessment and even more selling, you're effectively sitting at around a 4 percent annual cost. This means you may make a gross return on your hard-earned money of 8 percent or even 12 percent when the economy is good. However, you would be giving them 4 percent which could amount to a third or even half of your annual earnings.

The second kind of advisor is the registered investment advisor or fiduciary. This is a person you pay to give you advice and unbiased information which is untainted by any commission earning. Their job here is to answer your questions, give you straight-up answers about which investment streams are best for you without figuring in how they can benefit from this.

Using a fiduciary is not an option when you have many kinds of managed funds, especially within the 401K of your employer. Why is this? If you have a 401K plan, administered by an employer, the fund will already be managed. Therefore, you will likely not have an option to turn it over to a fiduciary.

However, if you are considering rolling over your 401K or other retirement instruments or if it is time to make other investment decisions outside of an employer's control, then it is a good time to get an unbiased, paid consultation from an independent fiduciary.

How do you find an independent fiduciary? Many firms have fiduciaries but you must make a request for an independent one. Vanguard, Schwab, Hightower and Strongholdfinancial.com, as of the publication of this book, have a team of fiduciaries.

Here's one final note on investing and this is the best advice I have for those trying to save for retirement. Purchase and read the book, *Money: Master the Game* by Tony Robbins. Many of the ideas I shared here come from this book and there are many dozens of other ideas there that could save you many thousands of dollars. If you don't have the time or the discipline to read all the details in this powerful book on investing, you can always get my review of the book by going to www.smallbizzoom.com.

End of Chapter Action Items

1. **Read this book**

   If you are not already in business but would like to be, read the 8th *Habit: From Effectiveness to Greatness* by Stephen R Covey. In the book, Stephen discusses identifying where your passion and skills meet another person's needs. This process could help you identify a thriving business opportunity.

2. **Get an independent evaluation of your fees instantly**

   If you have a 401K Plan as an investment, go to www. americasbest401K.com to have them evaluate your fees. Compare and consider whether making a change makes sense for your situation and your retirement goals.

3. **Figure out your retirement needs**

   Visit www.smallbizzoom.com to get my down and dirty retirement calculator tool.

4. **Get the advice of a fiduciary**

   Take the time to do your homework and locate a reasonably priced independent fiduciary. Read *Money: Master the Game* or read my review of that book. Either way, do some research on ways to build your retirement assets and get advice from a few financial advisors including taking all of this to a fiduciary. Once you have completed this process, you should be able to make a few informed decisions on how and where to invest your money and what you can expect to pay in terms of fees.

9 | Oxygen Rich Business Blood Flow

How to decrease risk, cut costs and streamline procedures when cash flow is low

*Never take your eyes off the cash flow because
it's the lifeblood of business*

–Richard Branson

When I was eighteen years old, as a reward for achieving the rank of Eagle Scout, my scoutmaster took me to the summit of Mt Rainier, at 14,410 feet. It was, to say the least, an exceedingly hard endeavor. What made it harder was my epilepsy. The intense physical effort that was required over two days to reach that summit created intense mental exertion. This, in turn, brought about a seizure unlike any other, right at the very summit!

I was unconscious and helpless at that summit and oxygen was hard to come by. My scoutmaster could not carry me off the mountain by himself. Thankfully, there were three Army Rangers who were climbing the mountain that day.

I awoke at some point to discover them carrying me down, about an hour into their rescue efforts. For three hours, I was not able to walk but gradually, I regained my strength, put my pack back on and trekked the rest of the way down that magnificent mountain.

It would be more than 20 years later, about a week after the miraculous brain surgery that cured my epilepsy, that I knew full well what I needed to do.

The seizure I endured on that mountain years ago meant I never got to see the summit that day. This mountain was now something I had to conquer. So, for a year, together with a team of climbers, I began training.

We climbed small peaks all over of the state and then took on Mt St. Helens (at only 8,366 feet now after exploding in 1980), Mt. Adams (12,280 feet) and Mt. Hood in Oregon (11,250 feet) in preparation. Add to that, vigorous workouts, other training, and preparation. It was about a year after my brain surgery that I went back to Mt Rainier.

The entire event was going to take place over a 48 hour period. It was because we had prepared, trained and persevered that we were successful in summiting on the morning of day two.

Running a business is very much like climbing a gigantic mountain. It requires time, great effort, education, perseverance through the rough times and making many wise business decisions along the way. As part of our preparations to climb, we had spent hours learning how to catch ourselves in a fall down a snowfield.

In business, you learn how to solve problems sometimes the hard way, and along the way, hopefully, you have continuing education or mentoring. In preparing for Mt Rainier, we learned best practices on how to breathe when oxygen was less than 40 percent of normal while working out hard. In business, you learn how to minimize expenses and closely monitor cash flow when sales are lean and cash is low.

In this chapter, you will learn ways to decrease your risks, cut your costs and streamline procedures in your business so that you are well prepared when your "oxygen" level (your cash flow) is below a comfortable, sustainable level.

CASH FLOW IS KING

Let me start by talking about Cash Flow, the board game (and now app) created by Robert Kiyosaki. I first played it, many years ago, before getting into business as an independent CPA. Cash flow is awesome and I highly recommend you play this game with as many people as you can.

This game teaches you that it is not necessarily the price of your investments that is important but the positive or negative cash flow that these investments produce consistently.

If you are in business as a hobby and have other steady streams of cash flow to support your hobby, all is well. However, if you depend on your business for your daily expenses, then you need to take action to create predictable, positive cash flow in your business. Regardless of the business you are in, cash flow is king.

One of my clients, a chiropractor, who began working independently about a year ago, learned this the hard way. After being in business for nine months, he came in for a consultation. We reviewed his "dire" financial situation. I quickly learned that about 75 percent of his "good earnings" were coming from what is called "3rd Party Insurance Claim" work. This refers to you providing services to a patient who has found themselves in great need of chiropractic care who is also suing an insurance company or another party for an accident or another claim.

When the lawsuit is finally concluded and the pay-out is made, all parties get paid a negotiated amount of the settlement or winnings. My client had a dozen third party claims awaiting payment but he had very little cash-paying customers outside of this. Without the needed daily cash inflows, his business was choking. His business's oxygen level was at about 5 percent.

The first thing we did was to change his focus to cash-paying work. He had to conduct specific activities to bring in cash-paying customers and then, as the big-ticket claims began to pay, he started the process of paying off credit cards and loans. Today, he is thriving, taking in only one third party claim at a time, alongside hundreds of cash and insurance paying customers.

> Remarkably, in setting the bar very high,
> I did not lose a single client.

This chiropractor also did two other note-worthy things to increase the cash flow in his business. The first was related to insurance. He chose to outsource his medical billing and made it a requirement that it had to be done on the day of service. He established detailed systems on collecting all of the necessary insurance information at the first service with the customer as well as required a customer deposit for co-pays.

The second thing the chiropractor did was to create a membership program, wherein many customers would get ongoing chiropractic wellness work done alongside excellent education and fitness training to stay healthier.

TWO CRITICAL CHANGES THAT HELPED ME

When the economy took a downward spiral in 2008, I made two critical changes to the systems in my business. The first one was to require all customers to pay at the time of service. This took an adjustment for my staff, my clients and for me because we tended to let things slide every once in a while. Remarkably, in setting the bar very high, I did not lose a single client.

I now have a system whereby business clients, who may have several transactions with me in any given month are set up for automatic bill payment and auto-debit accounts. I have an agreement in place with them to run ACH (Automated Clearing House) transactions on their account once a month for any fees owed. This process is streamlined and efficient, keeping me at near-zero accounts receivable. Before I did this, there were some months that I was running almost $85,000 in accounts receivable which is equivalent to over a month's worth of gross revenue.

The second critical change I made, in my public accounting firm, was to complete a thorough review of our business expenses. As an accountant, it has always been part of my job to find ways to cut overhead costs for my clients.

In 2008, I decided to do the same for my own firm. Since then, I have developed an extremely detailed method for helping my clients do the same. It starts with a detailed review of all expense accounts. We place the expenses into four categories for a minimum three month period:

i)   **required and necessary expenses**

This refers to expenses for which you are contractually bound. Some of these contracts may be negotiated, though often, they are not.

ii)   **discretionary and optional expenses**

This refers to expenses that can be removed, lowered or negotiated down - these need to be addressed.

iii) **revenue-generating expenses**

This refers to expenses, which if removed, will mean a loss of revenue. Typically, it includes things like advertising or some payroll expenses.

iv)   **the less costly alternative expenses**

This refers to expenses where you can do some comparison shopping, explore cost-cutting or reorganize your priorities so that you are minimizing costs.

Once we thoroughly review all expenses, we create a new target budget for the next three months, returning to review it together. It was these two changes alone which kept me in a positive cash flow position over the three year period 2008 until 2011. This was the time the economy had sunk and I began to lose dozens of clients, both corporations as well as individual tax clients. Today, we still enforce the "pay at the time of completed service" policy fully and carry less than $500 in accounts receivable month-to-month.

A construction company that I provide services to adopted a similar process. First, they streamlined their expenses following the methods I outlined above. Then, they changed their collection process. It is customary, in their industry, for bigger contracts to require a 50 percent down-payment for construction work to begin. The balance 50 percent is then collected on completion.

We modified their contracts, trained their sales and accounting staff. Today they get paid in full on completion and this is how they do it.

First, they collect the client's credit card or banking information at the time the contract is signed. Next, they have the client sign a collection agreement which simply states that they will pay 50 percent on contract signing, 25 percent at an agreed-upon midway completion status, 20 percent when the work is 90 percent complete and the final 5 percent when the inspection is done by the supervisor. That final 5 percent would either be paid in hand or an ACH debit on that day as agreed.

If the client does not meet the agreed target payment dates, then they would simply move their team on to another project which 99 percent of the time, gets them making a payment immediately. Their final rule is that, in order to get the team back on the job when an agreed-upon progress payment has not been made, they would need to pay 95 percent of the bill together with any late fees incurred. This process is always explicitly explained to their customers who very rarely disagree or break their contract.

End of Chapter Action Items

1. **Review your collection and payment policies**

    Take a look at the Customer Payment Policies, Accounts Receivable Reporting, collections procedures and payment options (cash, credit, etc) you have in practice. Comparison shop to see whether there are competitors with better terms and payment options. Ensure your sales procedures and contracts enforce payment terms that are effective. Establish systems within your business to monitor customer balances, receive payments, collect payments in a timely manner and to inform and train customers to pay when contractually obligated.

2. **Conduct a Cash Flow Review**

    If your cash-flow isn't consistent, predictable and positive, conduct a three-month cash flow evaluation, using the method I showed earlier, identifying ways you can reduce your cash outflows.

3. **Review all business expenses**

    Review these expenses, dividing them as described, and consider where changes can be made to create a positive impact.

STRATEGY #5

Skyrocketing Profitability

Come to terms with technology's place
in today's world and master it

10 | Technology is Your Friend

Using technology to automate, to save costs and to simplify

Technology is a useful servant but a dangerous master

–Christian Lous Lange

As a consultant and business owner, I constantly hear about the latest and best apps and gadgets available. Many are useless but there are some which are effective in streamlining cash flow, cutting expenses, generating greater revenues and saving you time.

The problem is that there are literally hundreds of these apps now and several phone carriers to consider.

The best way to proceed is to check out your app store for specific business apps that you might find useful such as auto mileage record keepers, charitable donation record keepers, expense record-keepers or banking apps.

YOUR PHONE CARRIER

One piece of technology that I changed during my 2008 review of business expenses was my phone carrier. I was using one of the big phone companies. We had five phone lines and a fair amount of long-distance calls which meant I had a monthly phone bill of about $300.

Today, I pay less than $100 a month. The cost of my hardware (the phones) went down from a whopping $35,000 to $1,000! We started using VOIP (Voice Over Internet Protocol) whereby you access the telephone lines through your internet connection.

We no longer have expensive service calls to repair our phone system. We never again have to pay thousands of dollars to upgrade the phone system. Our phone bill is far less than what the big phone companies are charging now for the same service.

We use an independent carrier who does not say "save a little money using VOIP" because VOIP is nearly free for them and they pass this on to us. We have a steady, reliable service and this is available to companies of any size. Check it out and pass the word along. You can find out my carrier's rates and compare against yours at www.getsoundline.com.

I know many small businesses that have gone straight to using cell phones which is typically pretty affordable. I would argue, first, to take a look at the cost of a VOIP which will enable you to use the phone through any internet connection. Second, take a close look at competitor rates for cell phone plans. You could save thousands of dollars through a diligent review of usage, functionality, number of units and shared payment plans (by staff who are using the phone for personal use too). There are also many useful apps now for things like monitoring activity, locations and uses of the cell phones by your employees.

THE MAGICJACK

Consider also the Magicjack. It is a device that plugs into a USB port on your computer (or a router) and has a standard phone jack into which any standard phone can be plugged.

This allows the user to make unlimited phone calls to the US and Canada. It also allows you to use your fax machine over the internet and is extremely affordable.

THE FAX MACHINE

While the fax machine is now a lesser-used option with the advent of email and other communication systems, it is still widely used in many industries. So, for those who still use faxes, make sure to use software that offers an ability to digitize the entire process. Such software can be purchased and integrated into many fax machines.

THE SCANNER

Are you using a printer for many of your critical documents? To save costs, consider using a printer that allows you to email directly to your clients, rather than print, mail or fax.

Instead of printing out all the documents that you need to send clients, consider scanning and emailing them instead.

We used to spend $8,000 annually on printer ink and paper to prepare all the tax returns and those requisite copies. Today, we scan and email those same files, reducing our printing costs to just below $1,000 annually!

CUTTING COSTS

There are many useful apps available, either for free or for a nominal fee. Spend time to educate yourself and your staff so that you can avoid spending company dollars when you could use these apps to plan your spending more efficiently and at a lower cost.

Take, for example, the issue of security. There are now tools and apps for you to monitor your buildings and obtain enhance security. These devices or apps do not require a monthly fee for these monitoring activities. You have the benefit of real-time information on any activity as well as the ability to automate or personally respond to potential intruders, right from your phone.

If your company spends a large amount of money on computer hardware and software, you need to keep abreast of developments that can potentially reduce your fees.

i) iPads and cell phones, relatively inexpensive, can now replace the use of computers;

ii) a centralized server can eliminate hard drives at every work station;

iii) online software subscriptions and POS systems, along with inexpensive remote backup services can eliminate the need for big servers and computer terminals while increasing security and cash in hand;

iv) wireless networks are replacing and simplifying networking;

v) focused efforts to use email, integrated apps and texting are decreasing mailing and faxing needs which are more costly;

vi) a good review of network administration options (including various kinds of outsourcing options) are eliminating or heavily reducing computer support and networking requirements;

vii) another improvement has been the use of technology to automate many procedures such as bookkeeping, typing, phone answering, marketing activities and much more.

> One way in which technology can save you thousands of dollars is by hiring people to work from home.

Entire books have been written just on technology alone. This is, however, a good start for any business thinking of cutting costs and streamlining their operations.

SHOULD YOU OUTSOURCE?

Could your business utilize any aspect of outsourcing whether it is using a specialized external contractor locally or for technology maintenance?

Could you consider outsourcing to reduce your labor or overhead costs such as accounting and the work done by your receptionist?

Today, I no longer have a marketing person. I spend about $20,000 annually in various outsourcing activities such as to manage our social media channels, to create website content on a regular basis and to develop marketing materials. I used to pay for one marketing position at a loaded annual cost of $69,600.

One way in which technology can save you thousands of dollars is by hiring people to work from home. This used to be very hard to manage but not any longer. Technological advances have now made it easier to ensure that your staff, who access and use any type of electronic device to do their work, can be monitored. The common misconception about these hires is that you need to pay these staff more since they are independent contractors in many cases. This is false.

The way to approach this is from the perspective of the person hired:-

i) they have the ability to save time and travel costs;

ii) if they work independently, they also save on payroll taxes;

iii) if they do not need benefits (let's say that their spouse covers them), they can cut that shared cost out;

iv) they are also able to write off home office expenses, home office supplies (which they can also use for personal use simultaneously), cell phone, travel and internet expenses directly against their income, further reducing their tax liability with the IRS; and

v) they have the added convenience of choosing their hours (in most cases), being at home with the kids and family (if desired or needed) and many other perks.

This combination of benefits means that they can be compensated less and the employer can save money in multiple ways. Many employers today provide much of the resources necessary for an employee to succeed when working from home. They are still able to save many thousands annually by renting less space, paying fewer taxes and lowering administrative or direct costs absorbed by the external hires.

COMPETITION IS YOUR WINNING HAND

When you're playing poker, a full house is a fabulous hand. It's much better than three-of-a-kind or two pairs of any number or suit. However, if the player across you has a flush in their hand, your full house will mean nothing. You will lose.

In business, every financial aspect of your company can be viewed as a poker hand. The good news, however, is that frequently, you can win when others compete against you.

Take, for instance, outsourcing your computer technology and networking needs. Let's say, that you currently have a part-time IT guy. You pay him $2,000 a month to look after your machines and company network. You decide to outsource and get three outsiders to bid for the work.

To make this a smooth apples-to-apples comparison, you diligently prepare a summary of everything that is needed to successfully manage your network and put it out there to be bid on. Whether it's a local provider or an international one (this might be needed if you are looking for remote access), you get at least three bids (maybe a few more) and then conduct a close comparison of their offerings.

You might be surprised at the outcome. There are many networking companies that employ top quality technical staff who look after dozens of companies simultaneously, thus spreading their costs across multiple revenue streams. They have a winning hand, and by allowing them to compete for your business, you get the best deal.

What aspect of your business do you think you can outsource? For some, the question may be answered by considering what aspects cannot be outsourced. Whether it is technology, accounting, reception services, administrative tasks, marketing activities, order fulfillment, warehousing, shipping, selling or production ... the possibilities are endless.

Take a look at all the expenses in your business. Rather than assume that outsourcing will not work for you, carry out an internet search of companies that provide the services you currently complete in-house. Create an effective summary of exactly what needs to be done and allow competition to play its part. Do due diligence on final candidates, of course.

Then, where possible, test and measure your results. If it's a winning relationship, you could win big. There are a number of positive consequences to such activity such as improved performance, better service, more efficient output, higher quality finished products, more freedom and less stress to you and others within your company as well as the ability to scale.

End of Chapter Action Items

1. **Review potential apps you can use in your business**

   Check out your cell phone's App Store for a wide variety of apps that could make bookkeeping, taxes, mileage tracking, expense tracking and other industry-specific activities easier, faster and more accurate.

2. **Use VOIP**

   Consider switching to VOIP and review the options available because this could save you thousands a year.

3. **Review your cell phone plan**

   Do an analysis on all aspects of your plan including the rate you're paying, staff usage, what you need and what you don't, what competitors are offering, the number of lines you need, what tools are available to monitor employee usage and productivity on the job, etc.

11 | Change is Happening at an Ever-Increasing Rate

How will you manage it?

*The secret of change is to focus all of your energy,
not on fighting the old but on building the new*

–Socrates

I remember attending a seminar once that was put on by professionals in my industry. They were educating us on how to ensure the integrity and security of our data. In the accounting and tax world, this is a big issue with significant consequences for not being up-to-date.

The presenter explained how things had progressed over the last twenty years and how technology was changing the way we do things. Interestingly, he also discussed the future of technology, going on to make a comment I will never forget. He said, "In today's world, change is ongoing, and all must adapt or fail. The way to encourage others to change quickly is to help them understand that the real issue is not the change we are making today. The real issue is the rate at which change is happening. If you want to be in business, employed, alive, in the coming years, you must adapt to change which is always going to be coming faster at us."

If the rate of change is ever-increasing, as entrepreneurs in a vicious and competitive world, we will survive not by simply embracing change but by excelling in a changing environment.

Be the creator of change within your industry. Be the innovative creator of newer and faster ways of doing things. Streamline your business for change and take the bull by the horns. We have been doing that for several years now in our firm. From the adoption of many technological advances to outsourcing and streamlining our operations and the use of technology to create automated processes in bookkeeping, we are in some ways leading change.

On top of our efforts to educate ourselves, we provide this same education to our clients across diverse industries. We demand changes of our software providers and their development teams, including the developers of QuickBooks, Microsoft and our complex tax software, all of whom take our advice and ideas seriously and even give us credit for these ideas.

THE FUTURE IS BRIGHTER THAN YOU THINK

Do you know what is great about technology? From a financial standpoint, it is the fact that while the cost of technology is decreasing, its capacity is expanding exponentially.

What this means for you and me is that we will likely have a greater quality of life in the future for even less than what it costs today. Learning and adopting the technologies and trends, as they surface, could mean great opportunities for your business and lifestyle. The time to pay attention to them is right now.

> *The best way to predict the future is to invent it*
> - Alan Kay

Take, for example, burn treatment. Every ten minutes in America, someone is horribly burned. Check out the story of Matt Uram on YouTube. He was next to a bonfire when someone threw gasoline on it, burning his right arm and the right side of his head and face. Normally, he would have gone to a hospital's burn unit and endured up to a month of twice-daily agonizing treatments which would have left him scarred for life.

Instead, he had a team of specialists work on a new technique where a layer of healthy cells, from an unburned patch of his skin, was harvested. They were not using cadaver skin. These cells were cultured after which a solution containing Matt's stem cells was then gently painted on his wounds using a spray gun. Three days later, Matt's arms and face were completely healed with barely a visible scar.

It may sound unbelievable but this actually took place in Pittsburgh a few years ago. The medical community is going through a transformation like never before. They now have "bio-pens" in Europe and Australia that draw stem cells and allow them to conduct healing procedures in many different ways.

Take also, nano-technology, which has the ability to revolutionize the way we diagnose and treat diseases in people. Add to this, robotic surgery, stem cell organ transplants and other advances in medicine. In a recent speech I heard, the topic discussed was the concept of living forever. Stay with me on this. The researcher explained that today, with the perfect combination of vitamins, super healthy eating and healthy living, he planned to live long enough for the medical community to develop nano-technology which would cure any disease he had before it could mortally wound him. Additionally, further technological advances would allow the replacement of any body part as they wear out. This researcher was genuine and knowledgeable in his assessment that technology would keep him alive indefinitely.

The future brings a world where cars drive without human beings, where order fulfillment warehouses are fully robotic and automated and where voice and activity recognition tools will behave like human beings in responding to us. The world of the future will have a dozen new forms of energy production all of which are far cheaper than today's options. Gasoline engines, electronics as we know them and solar energy will be non-existent or thousands of times more efficient.

> In fact, the world today provides opportunities to entrepreneurs that were never before available.
> Your business can manufacture your products overseas as much as you can in your living room.

Clean water is a somewhat scarce resource on earth, especially in third world countries and communities that depend on dams and rivers which are being overused by millions of people in large cities and farming districts. Yet, technology is on the verge of making clean and pure water a fully accessible resource to all.

Things are changing rapidly in nearly every possible way and it will impact every industry. Why is this? It is because you and I demand it. We not only embrace it but we will provide our clients with better and cheaper options as these developments occur.

Look at 3-D printer technology. This alone will revolutionize every form of production, construction, engineering and the kind of products being made. This type of printer can use at least 200 different liquefied materials including plastic, glass, ceramic, titanium, nylon, chocolate and even living cells.

What can you make with such materials which are designed on a computer? The better question is, what can't you make with them? These 3-D printers will soon be in every home and be as common as the laptop or iPad. How do you think that will impact manufacturing and production globally?

Look at food. Today, we plant on acres of land. Tomorrow, we plant in science labs, vertically. Tomorrow's world will use in-vitro cloning of muscle tissue in computerized factories – at a lower cost, with high nutritional quality, and without environmental impact. No more insecticides. No more nitrogen pollution. No more the need to kill animals for protein. Wow!

Let's consider how all of this comes together. Ten years ago, the internet connected 500 million people. Today, it connects over two billion. Within six years, experts estimate another three billion will be joining the web, making that a total of five billion people. Imagine the power of that much connected and unleashed creativity across the planet.

Now, consider the Internet of Things (IoT). Computers and sensors are embedded in everyday objects, transmitting messages back and forth to one another. Machines are connected to other machines, which in turn, are connecting us and uniting everything in one powerful global network. The use of this technology and 3-D printing will be how the internet is transformed and expanded upon beyond our wildest dreams.

The world of nanotechnology will revolutionize medical practices and forever change every single profession within the medical industry. How will technology affect service providers, such as real estate agents, janitors, accountants, production workers and those in computer science? In a few short years, the world we will live in may not even be recognizable to us.

Look at the vast opportunities in energy. We are moving from oil to bio-fuels and – the grand slam winner – solar energy. According to inventor and futurist, Ray Kurzweil, all of the world's energy needs can be met with $1/10,000^{th}$ of the sunlight that falls on the Earth each day.

Ray predicts that, in just a few years, the cost of capturing and storing that power will be less than the cost of oil and coal. Then, imagine a world revolutionized by the power that fision (chemical technology to separate atoms which is similar to the fusion bomb of earlier years) will create. Once this technology is developed, it will trump all forms of energy development known at this time.

What will be next? How will the growth of the internet and technology affect communication? Just a few short years ago, in 1991 to be exact, we were introduced to a new form of communication called email, a commodity even the President of the United States did not have.

Nowadays, the cell phone that an Amazonian tribesman carries around the jungle has more instant computing power than the US President had at his disposal then. He can go online to buy supplies for his cows, pay his bills, transfer money in his bank account and communicate with anyone in the world who has a similar device. He can translate languages on demand as well as access free courses from Yale or MIT. We're living in a wholly different place now and this is only the beginning.

Yes, this is only the beginning of communication. Today, the cell phone has more intelligence than anyone's brain. We'll soon be moving from cell phones to wearables and then on to implantable devices that will, of all things, feed our brains. Is this possible?

Just think about the prospect that you soon won't have to read this book. You could just upload its contents into your brain. Are we stretching it to say that the world will someday allow you to upload your mind, thoughts or personality to the cloud to be preserved forever?

I believe there will still be a place for the entrepreneur in our future world. In fact, the world today provides opportunities to entrepreneurs that were never before available. Your business can manufacture your products overseas as much as you can in your living room. You can keep your warehouse regionally or build "just-in-time" what is requested. Retail can be conducted electronically, on-demand and order fulfillment can be automated. You can sell anything you want to anyone around the world. You only need to be good at social media and Google, networking and organization in order to develop a multi-million dollar company. However, ignore technology and you will be sitting with a sign on a street corner begging for cheap booze. So, what then is the solution to dealing with change?

Be an agent of change. Review every aspect of your business. Look deeply at all aspects of your industry. Be the one who dares to take the next step in technology. Be the one who then creates or demands the creation of new, better uses of technology.

End of Chapter Action Items

1. **Think about how you can take advantage of what's available**

    Are your products and services in danger of becoming irrelevant because of technological changes? What can you do to lead change or take advantage of these advances to revolutionize your industry? Herein lie the real rewards for the entrepreneur.

Cover your ASSets

Understand taxes, the legal system and
the best corporate vehicles that support you

12 | This Enemy Can Take You Down!

Audit triggers to be aware of, how to prevent an audit and dealing with being audited

Winning is the science of being totally prepared

–George Allen, Sr

I woke up one morning quite excited to go to work. This was right after the business tax deadline in April 1999. I was the happy owner of my own business and still enjoying the excitement that it brings.

At the office, I was quickly reviewing emails, intending to spend the rest of my day on a project for a valued client, when I read an email from a doctor-client of mine for whom I provided accounting and tax services. The email headline read, "I'M GETTING AUDITED BY THE IRS!"

That was the first audit I would undergo with a client. I am certain that I was more scared than he was, as we prepared for the day that the IRS would come in and proceed to rip us apart! I couldn't sleep at all the night before the auditor was scheduled to arrive.

I worked hard, from every angle, for my client. I spent three days trudging through all kinds of documents, sitting right beside that auditor. I've since learned that sitting with the auditor is not as effective as allowing them to get on with their job.

In the end, my client came out clean except for one error which turned out to be my fault. I had made a deduction for a bad debt on his cash-basis tax return which was not allowed. Being embarrassed does not even begin to describe how I felt but it was a learning experience for me. I paid my client's penalty in full and have yet to make this mistake again.

Experiences like this are the reason why you should always consult a seasoned professional. We all learn from mistakes but when you are being audited, you want to work with someone who has learned all the right lessons about this. While the IRS is forthcoming with many of its rules and regulations, there is selected information that the IRS simply will not inform you about.

WHAT TRIGGERS AN AUDIT?

You simply cannot fully protect yourself from having your tax return examined and there are a few key tax issues you need to be aware of when preparing your return. For example, there are some things that can trigger an audit such as reporting more expenses than income. In determining whether a tax return should be audited, many factors can come into play.

> If you have been selected for an IRS audit, do not panic. You will have the opportunity to state your side of the case.

These include things like the losses you're making from year to year, unusual and large deductions that may appear questionable and third-party referrals.

(1) Higher-income earners

Unfortunately, these people are, on a ten to one basis, more likely to get audited than others. This is simply because they have more complex returns which means more opportunity for error.

(2) Sole proprietors and landlords

If you are self-employed or are getting rental income, a red flag may be embedded in your return. Unlike wage earners, sole proprietors and landlords can report income and expenses at their discretion. This is especially relevant given that there are times they may receive cash or unreported payments from their clients or customers. Incorporation is an easy resolution to this problem because corporations are one-thirteenth as likely to get audited as sole-proprietorships.

(3) Questionable and/or large deductions

Deductions are also reviewed to ensure that they are in line with reported income. For example, it may be reasonable to have $3,000 in meal expenses deducted if you make $3,000,000 in revenues. It will not be so reasonable if you're making only $100,000 in revenues.

When preparing your tax return, ask yourself how reasonable your expenses are and whether they are customary in your line of work.

For example, does your company really need to pay excessive amounts in meals and entertainment costs if you run a dog-trainer business? Maybe, maybe not. Either way, your tax return has to first pass the "smell test" to avoid an audit.

(4) Underreporting income

This is an instant audit trigger. The IRS ensures taxpayers' compliance through its Automated Underreporting Program. This program matches the income reported on the federal income tax return to information obtained from third parties, such as employers and financial institutions.

If there is a mismatch, you will receive a notice from the IRS informing you of an additional tax assessment, and perhaps, even an audit.

Take note, though, that while the IRS is forthcoming about its automated underreporting program, penalties assessed can be waived if you can show reasonable cause.

The good news is that every individual receives a one-time free waiver of penalties from the IRS. No exceptions.

WHAT DO YOU DO WHEN YOU ARE AUDITED?

(1) Know your rights

If you have been selected for an IRS audit, do not panic. You will have the opportunity to state your side of the case. Realize that there are many ways you can substantiate items on your tax return other than canceled checks or receipts.

Examiners allow the reconstruction of financial documents. Examiners also accept, to some extent, oral testimony. Additionally, in recent years, technological advances have resulted in other options through which you can prove your expenses.

(2) Seek tax representation

This is important. In most cases, the IRS wants to deal directly with the taxpayer because they find that taxpayer representatives often stall the process. However, tax representatives can often help you navigate through this process and may be more likely to obtain favorable results.

(3) Be open to negotiate and agree on things quickly

In a civil audit, the examiner's primary objective is to close the report in a timely manner and have the taxpayer agree with the IRS positions, usually referred to as an agreed report.

This is typically viewed favorably if it can be done within a reasonable time period. It is for this reason that an examiner may be willing to negotiate certain disputed items in your favor in order to finalize things quickly and prepare an agreed report.

(4) Establish a good rapport with your tax agent

It is important for you to establish a good rapport with your agent and to be able to substantiate most of the disputed or questionable items on your return.

If you do so, the examiner may be willing to take oral testimony to prove other questionable areas. This may be where a third party representative may be helpful.

(5) Do not take a 'no' for an answer

There is always a little room to reduce your tax liability. If you do not like your examination's outcome, request to have your case reviewed by the supervisor of that person or the Appeals Division.

Appeals are a viable option for a taxpayer to resolve difficulties within the IRS. Sometimes, the examiner may overlook some tax areas because of his haste to close the examination. Appealing allows the taxpayer to change the decision received.

Be persistent about educating yourself about your rights prior to any audit. This will work in your favor although the best strategy anyone can have is to avoid an audit in the first place.

End of Chapter Action Items

1. **Review our checklist for becoming audit-proof**

   Go through all the steps, outlined in our checklist on becoming audit-proof. Find it at:

   http://www.actiontaxteam.com/services/audit-proof/#&panel1-1.

2. **If you find out that you're getting audited**

   Do not panic. Send me that letter and we will schedule an appointment with you to discuss the process, a strategy, and anticipated outcomes. If it proves necessary, we can also postpone the date of the audit in order to prepare ourselves adequately. Most importantly, do not attempt to represent yourself in a face-to-face audit with the IRS.

9 Things You May Not Know About the IRS

#1 The IRS Fails to Collect Billions of Taxes Owed Every Year

In recent years, the number of uncollected tax dollars reached $350 billion! Whether you believe that this unclaimed money should be used for certain programs or to simply pay down our existing national debt, this is money that Americans are not paying as they should be. (This number is estimated to be low because the IRS depends on people to self-report and provide an estimate as to what they owe).

#2 The IRS Has 10 Years to Collect Taxes Owed

When taxes are due on your return, you are required to pay the entire balance by April 15th in addition to possibly being required to make estimated tax payments. Penalties and interest charges accrue on the owing balance. However, after 10 years, the IRS is unable to collect from you. You will then be off the hook!

The IRS must not have been able to get a single collection within those 10 years or time starts running again.

#3 The IRS Is Not Really Interested in Seizing Property

If you have gotten behind in paying taxes and are dealing with a collection agent, you may find him threatening to seize your property and assets. However, this isn't really their goal. This is simply a threat they like to make to get you moving.

Bank accounts are easy to seize and the IRS will do it. However, seizing your property and then reselling it does not bring in much of a return for the hours and money spent. Your wages can also be garnished easily. This is something they will do if you continue to ignore their requests to pay back money owed long enough.

#4 The IRS (Or Their Computers, At Least) Do Make Mistakes

Just because the IRS says that you owe money does not necessarily mean it is so. The best thing to do when you have received an audit notice (especially if you believe it is one that can be easily proven wrong) is to move forward with getting it amended.

One of our clients received a CP-2000 audit notice, claiming she failed to report over $44,500 in income. It was attached to a $16,000 tax bill plus fees. However, it turned out that the IRS had mistakenly counted a $445.00 1099MISC-form from a client as a $44,500 1099MISC-form. With a little help from our firm, it was cleaned up without owing a dime.

#5 If You Work, the Earned Income Tax Credit (EITC) Can Work In Your Favour!

Since 1975, the EITC has helped workers with low or moderate incomes to get a tax break each year. Four out of five eligible workers claim EITC but the IRS wants everyone who is eligible to claim this credit.

Here are some things you should know about this valuable credit:

1. **Review your eligibility**
   If you worked and earned under $52,427 in 2016, you may qualify for EITC. If your financial or family situation has changed, you should review the EITC eligibility rules. You might qualify for EITC this year even if you didn't in past years. If you qualify for EITC, you must file a federal income tax return and claim the credit to receive this. This is true even if you are not otherwise required to file a tax return.

Do not make a guess about your EITC eligibility. Use the EITC Assistant tool on IRS.gov. This tool helps you find out if you qualify and provides an estimate of the amount of your EITC.

2. **Know the Rules**
    You need to understand the rules as to whether you qualify before you claim the EITC. It's important that you get this right. Here are some factors you should consider:
    (i)   your filing status cannot be "Married Filing Separately";

    (ii) you must have a Social Security number that is valid for employment for yourself, your spouse (if married) and any qualifying child listed on your tax return;

    (iii) you must have earned income. This includes earnings from working for someone else as well as working for yourself;

    (iv) to qualify, you may be either married or single, with or without children. If you do not have children, you must also meet age, residency and dependency rules. If you have a child who lived with you for more than six months in 2014, the child must meet age, residency, relationship and the joint return rules in order to qualify; and

    (v)   if you are a member of the US Armed Forces serving in a combat zone, special rules apply.

3. **Lower Your Tax or Get A Refund**
    The EITC reduces your federal tax and can result in a refund. If you qualify, the credit could be worth up to $6,143. The average credit in 2015 was $2,407.

#6 The IRS Wants to Settle Cases Before They Go To Trial

IRS attorneys are burdened with large workloads. Tax Court judges have more cases than they can reasonably handle. It also costs the government a lot of money to prepare for and attend the trial. The IRS tries to keep it secret because revealing this would give the taxpayer an edge in settlement negotiations.

If the IRS knows you are prepared to go to trial, you have a much greater chance of getting a favorable settlement.

#7 IRS Officials Give Taxpayers The Wrong Answer More Than 30 Percent of the Time

They would love to keep this a secret but they can't. If you obtain an incorrect answer from an IRS agent, you are not able to rely on it to avoid an accuracy-related penalty unless you managed to get it in writing.

Note, however, that IRS officials are instructed not to provide written advice. So, do not call the IRS if you have anything but the most rudimentary tax question. Even a seemingly benign question like where a particular tax form should be mailed to can result in a possible wrong answer, which in turn, creates unnecessary havoc in your life.

#8 Many Entry-Level Auditors and Collection Agents Do Not Have Tax or Financial Backgrounds

When a taxpayer contacts the IRS about a problem, he may naturally assume that the person he is speaking with has a thorough grasp of tax law and IRS practice and procedure. Nothing could be further from the truth.

Many IRS personnel – especially collection officers who work in the Automated Collection System (ACS) – lack any financial background or training. However, as anyone who has ever spoken with an ACS official can tell you, this lack of expertise does not stop some of these officers from confidently advising taxpayers (and their representatives) as to what the law says, what the IRS procedure is and what the taxpayer should do to resolve the problem.

Many ACS officials regularly give bad advice to taxpayers and regularly misstate the law. At times, they may say whatever they believe will most likely get the taxpayer to pay the IRS. This is especially true when they are dealing directly with taxpayers. There is a very good reason for this.

ACS officials are advocates for the government's interests, not the taxpayer's interests. If those IRS officials had any respect for the Taxpayer Bill of Rights, they would tell taxpayers that they have a conflict of interest and that it is unethical for them to give substantive tax advice. Further, they would then suggest that the taxpayer seek the advice of a qualified CPA or IRS enrolled agent.

#9 The Squeaky Wheel Gets the Oil

Make enough ruckus and the IRS will accede to your demands. This *does not* mean if you have a frivolous or irrational position that the IRS will roll over and let you win. What it does mean is that if you have a reasonable argument and present that argument thoroughly with appropriate supporting documentation and references to legal precedent, the IRS will, more often than not, grant you the relief you request.

When I talk about ruckus here, I am referring to a vigorous, thorough and persistent presentation of a *meritorious* position. A good taxpayer representative will exhaust all administrative remedies available to obtain relief for his client. These remedies include, but are not limited to:

1. the full use of the Collection Due Process and Collection Appeals Programs;

2. the full use of the Taxpayer Advocate's office; and

3. if necessary, the solicitation of the involvement of the taxpayer's congressman.

The Six Things That Are Not Tax Deductible For Anyone

#1 The cost of your meals

Technically, only the client portion of such meals is tax-deductible. This is the reason you only receive a 50 percent deduction for meals and entertainment.

#2 Penalties

All IRS or State Agency penalties are not allowed to be deducted.

#3 Commuting costs

This refers to the cost of getting from home to work and back.

#4 Undocumented cash donations

Without corresponding receipts, cash donations will not be allowed as tax-deductible by the IRS.

#5 Political contributions

While your contribution may help your candidate get elected, such contributions made are not tax-deductible.

#6 Volunteer time

While you may deduct monetary donations, you cannot deduct for time contributions.

13 | Strike a Deal, a Big Deal

Why legal battlefields are your last resort - aim to resolve in other ways

Avoid lawsuits with all your might

–Jacob M Hanes

It was March 15th, 2006, the day of the corporate tax deadline. I got to work extra early and began reviewing our files and reports, looking for a big list of extensions that would need to be filed. I could not locate the list. When the staff began arriving at work, I asked my new manager how many extensions we had left to file.

"None," was her response, "we filed them all two days ago." I was shocked and happy at the same time. Yet, I knew there had to be more for me to do on this very busy day.

Finally, I decided to call my business coach. He listened intently to my concerns and then asked me to visit him briefly at his office, which happened to be another suite in our office building. I got there quickly, getting myself prepared for instructions on how to organize today's busy day. Instead, Kevin brought me to a new realization.

"Congratulations, Jake," he began, "You now have a real business. As we call it at ActionCoach, a business is 'a profitable entity that runs itself without you, an investment.'"

He went on to explain that, without my direct involvement, my business was a machine working as it should. He said, "Now, don't go in and bother the team. You'll mess things up! Just relax and let everyone do their thing as they are." I chuckled, thinking that this was certainly what I had in mind to do.

WHEN DISASTER STRIKES

"It is time for you to begin working on your vision," Kevin continued. My vision at the time was to have ten operating businesses running successfully. I knew it was now time to have fun! It was time to acquire a new business, which I then did. At the end of 2006, I finalized the acquisition of a new CPA firm in a nearby city.

Much like a rollercoaster, however, things went up and also back down. The economy was not the only reason why. For a period of one year, I transitioned and began to take ownership of that new company, only to arrive at the start of another tax season in 2008.

I found my customers leaving in droves at my new firm. Four of my five staff walked out over a period of a week. Oddly enough, I found a competitor of mine trying to lease space right next to my office building. I had complaints from my clients coming at me through the Washington State Board of Accountancy. Then, shockingly, I discovered an ex-staff had opened a competing firm right down the street from my office, in the name of my company, and they were contacting and persuading my clients to move to them. This was not even the worst of it!

> The previous owner broke her covenant not to compete, stole my business and attempted to overtake me.

I soon found out that the person I acquired the firm from was stealing clients she had sold to me when she left for Colorado. She was telling my clients to file complaints against me and she was the one who helped the competitor open his firm down the street in my company name. This was a challenge of epic proportions.

It was the most intense and stressful experience I had ever suffered. To make a very long story short, a legal battle ensued over the next 18 months. In the end, I managed to get that competitor's office closed and regained many of the clients I lost. While that solved some of the problems, that in itself was not enough for me.

The previous owner broke her covenant not to compete, stole my business and attempted to overtake me. With 21 months of legal battle behind me and still continuing, my seizures began to get worse. I spent eight weeks battling more than 500 seizures, forcing me to postpone my court date.

At that time, the "very good" defense attorney (I can say that now though I had a true hatred for him then) filed yet another Motion to Dismiss the case against me. There were already four motions before this, leaving the judge who had given us many concessions quite irritated.

With this new motion, however, coupled with my requests for postponements, I was confronted with the judge's appalling about-face. Within minutes, I was sitting in that Superior Courtroom wondering how my case was now suddenly dropped!

AVOID LAWSUITS WITH ALL YOUR MIGHT

Let me tell you what I learned from that. You may think you have a strong case. You may even think you will most certainly win lots of money in court. You get bold and angry and hire an attorney.

However, I ended up losing more than $240,000 in legal fees and I did not get any recompense for the theft of nearly 200 clients. Your case may not be the same as mine and you may have strong evidence and a strong contract. I thought I had the same too.

What I have learned from this experience is that the only winners in any legal process are the attorneys. If you have a strong legal standing and there are ways for you to settle the dispute with the other party outside of the legal process, do so.

The stress, anguish, cost and time involved are just not worth it. Find a way to settle things quickly because even if you have been wronged, need to be repaid your losses or believe you could win your case, the legal process is not about who is right or wrong.

It is about good litigation, what precedents have already been set before your case and emotion. The deck is stacked against you in so many ways.

How do you justify the potential loss of your winnings? Calculate the legal fees you'll save. Then calculate all of the other costs of your time, your health, your sanity and peace of mind. Since that legal battle, I have had conversations with more than 100 people who have gone through legal battles. The right thing - settling things out of court quickly - has typically been done only 1 percent of the time. It is just not worth it.

End of Chapter Action Items

1. **What do you do if you are considering getting involved in a legal battle?**

   Do not see an attorney immediately. If you truly want to resolve the conflict with less cost, develop a plan of action and communicate this with a few trusted advisors. Do this so you can create a third alternative, one that will serve both parties. Look to create a win/win situation.

14 | You Didn't Sign the Pre-Nup?!

Build a deep, trusted relationship and take the requisite care or avoid it altogether

Trust is like an eraser -
it gets smaller and smaller after every mistake

–Anonymous

When I share with my clients the lessons learned from the more than 100 different legal cases I have been involved in personally or professionally, there is one reason, more than any other, for why many legal battles occur. Can you guess what that reason is? Bad partnerships.

Two years after my legal case was dropped, I was sitting across from a very angry construction business owner. He had invested more than $100,000 of his own money, into keeping his business afloat, over a five year period.

He was working, like a horse, six days a week during the nine busy months of the year and still stayed busy during the three slower months. He had not taken a single dime out of the business because it was always a case of either paying the employees or paying the partners. Every business owner knows who wins that contest!

As he sat across the table from me, sharing all the details of what he had been through and what he had learned, my past was rearing up in my mind and I was finding it hard to contain my own anger. This honest, hard-working construction worker had been defrauded by his partner by more than $400,000 over those five years!

Partnerships gone wrong are the reason for more than 85 percent of all business lawsuits.

The books were cooked and he was reeling. Legal action was the only possible remedy, in his eyes, and frankly, in mine too. I shared my story with him. As I did, I began to give him other options for avoiding a long, drawn-out legal battle so that he could still win and keep his business alive. Within a couple of hours, we had put together an amazingly detailed plan. He went to work on it over the next three months, with full vigor.

Four months after we first met, he came into my office unannounced, sat down and thanked me profusely for helping him work through all of the details. He managed to secure thousands of

his assets, secured the balance in the corporate accounts, retained every employee (except the bookkeeper who helped defraud him), paid $24,000 in back taxes and then completely closed out the other partner (who was now out of a job and plagued by a bad reputation) with $50,000 in debt to be paid back.

Partnerships gone wrong are the reason for more than 85 percent of all business lawsuits. Had this construction business owner gone down the legal route, not only would his resources (time, energy and cash) have been sucked up but he would have likely either won the case with nothing to take from the partner or lost his legal battle.

POTENTIAL ALTERNATIVES

Are there alternatives to partnerships? Yes, there are. My suggestion is that you do not get into a partnership. If you're in a situation where one partner has the money and the other has the skill (which is often the case), simply provide compensation to the skilled party.

Alternatively, explore Notes Receivable, which are assets of a company, bank or other organization that holds a promissory note from another party. The skilled person can create this Note Receivable with the partner at a mutually agreed-upon rate of return.

THINGS TO CONSIDER IF YOU ARE ALREADY IN A PARTNERSHIP

Here are two questions you should address in such a situation:

1) How do you protect yourself and each other?

2) How do you resolve differences and conflicts that arise?

(1) Draw up a detailed Partnership Agreement

Your Partnership Agreement should outline in detail how disputes will be resolved. It should detail the valuation and method used to determine the way a partner leaves as well as the amount he will receive on departure. Research how these may occur with examples you may find online. Share this with your attorney, giving him these examples and your notes so he is aware of your objectives. Identify who will be responsible for taxes, debts and operations should the business dissolve.

If one partner should walk away, identify the process for how they should be removed from the business. If one partner defrauds the others, identify the process for resolution. This is especially important in a case where there is no skin in the game (ie one partner has not invested money from the start).

147

(2) Identify how new partners are brought in

Be clear in your Partnership Agreement about how new partners will be allowed to buy into the business.

(3) Be clear about each partner's role

Look online for a detailed organization chart for a business. Look at all the roles a business has to fill and put each partner's name in the segments they will be responsible for. Write out in detail the expectations for each role in the form of a job description. Make sure that each partner then signs off on their roles and responsibilities.

(4) Be clear about the money

Depending upon the roles, activities, risks, and investments each partner is taking on, write out clear compensation details. There should be two documents, signed by all parties, that provide details on things like:

- how you will be compensated - base salary, bonuses, periodic draws (if any);
- will the company or the partners be responsible for their tax liabilities on profits earned? This is especially critical if draws are not taken or cash out is low but taxes are high;
- if money is needed for significant company purchases, will this be handled as a loan from a shareholder, a contribution by a shareholder, an increase in ownership to credit them for their equity contribution or something else?

(5) Hire a business coach

It may not seem like it but this is the most important thing to do. A business coach should be kept on board for the first twelve months, at the very least. It will make a huge difference to have this third party around to bounce off concerns and 'newlywed' bugs as you and your partners enter this 'marriage'.

A good coach will help create clear communication channels, quickly and equitably resolve disputes, and as an added bonus, help the business grow. Doing this will solve many problems. However, if this is simply not an option, go to your CPA, attorney, any colleague with lots of business experience or just anyone who you can engage to act as your intermediary with your partners.

In my firm, I act as an intermediary for a few different partnerships right now. Not only am I an independent third party who can review both sides of the story in order to come up with a reasonable third alternative, but I also insist that they have my firm do their books. In this way, I know the money is being properly distributed, the taxes and bills are being paid, and the partners are being compensated exactly as agreed upon.

So, while I suggest you refrain from choosing to run your business as a partnership, if this is what you have done or choose to do, you will be able to protect yourself, the business, your clients and other stakeholders if you follow these procedures.

End of Chapter Action Items

1. **If you are in a partnership of any kind**

   If you find that the procedures above are not done, communicate openly with the partners and create them. Have them reviewed by a third party, signed off by all partners and notarized. Begin creating business systems or employ a business coach to clearly monitor each partner's adherence to the agreed-upon practices and roles of all involved.

STRATEGY #7

Envision Your Dream Team

Towards dreaming big and getting the right people on board in a sustainable way

15 | Manage Systems, Lead People

Basic HR infrastructure, legal compliance and establishing good people practices

by Bill George

Human Resources isn't a thing we do.
It's the thing that runs our business

–Steve Wynn, Wynn Las Vegas

A s the owner of a small business, you turned a dream into a reality. You found a way to deliver a product or service that met the needs of your customers, charged a competitive rate and built a business from the proceeds. When demand grew, you found it necessary to add employees. Along with those employees came the associated managerial responsibilities and employment implications.

If your business is smaller-sized, with less than 50 employees, you probably have not hired someone to specifically address human resources (HR) management within your firm. More than likely, as the business owner, you have taken this role on yourself. This chapter is included to provide greater insight into the essential elements of HR management for the small business owner and includes basic HR infrastructure, legal compliance as well as where to find information and resources to establish a foundation for good people practices.

> Good advertising requires that you consider your intended audience and how best to attract them.

Given the wide variety in the types of businesses and owners who are represented in the readership of this book, there will be HR matters that are unique to your business that the scope of this chapter does not address.

In that case, a rigorous internet search or a discussion with an HR consultant, offered through a business association membership or employment law firm, may be time and money well spent.

RECRUITMENT AND RETENTION

Regardless of external market conditions, staffing your organization always takes effort and can pose a significant challenge. However, there are process fundamentals that, if followed, will result in better outcomes, both in terms of the election and retention of the kind of people you want to attract to your business.

The term "process control" (used widely in manufacturing industries to assure product conformance to quality standards) also has direct application for applying best practices in the finding and retaining of qualified employment candidates.

1. **Prepare A Job Description**

   The process begins with a well-written job description. Crafting a written job description allows you to clearly define the job title, duties, qualifications, experience, education and certifications you are looking for, in the ideal candidate for the position.

This job description serves as the main body of the job posting used to attract candidates, serves as a guide for preparing interview questions and provides a documented reference for setting performance goals and measuring employee conformance to performance standards.

Sample job descriptions, some at no cost, can be found on the internet. Check out *Indeed* for employers at www.indeed.com.

2. Post The Job

This is the next step in the process. With the job description written, you are ready to post your requirements. Keep in mind that a job posting is really a specialized advertisement to attract employment candidates.

Good advertising requires that you consider your intended audience and how best to attract them to consider your firm. You also need to consider what forms of media the candidate is likely to pay attention to.

For instance, a business with a sign viewed by hundreds of motorists daily may post, "we are hiring, inquire within". A business needing a group of construction workers for a major project may place an advertisement on a sports radio station. A firm looking for a candidate to fill a professional role may do a few things. It may post the opening on the company website, send a notification via a blog post or bulletin board announcement to professionals via social media or utilize a national job posting site that can provide a host of services on platforms such as LinkedIn, Indeed, Monster, Zip Recruiter, Career Builder, Glassdoor, etc.

Determining the "sweet spot" for successful recruiting may require a bit of trial and error. However, like any process you are trying to control, you make adjustments, learn what works and refine your approach until it returns consistent and effective results.

Other worthwhile approaches to recruiting that may not require the outlay of any funds include:

- Employee Referrals – Send an email to your team and invite them to refer any qualified friends or contacts. Alternatively, post the requirement on the company bulletin board or newsletter;
- State Employment Services – All states offer employment services and will post your requirement to their database of available jobs. You can typically fax or call in with the information;
- College Career Services – Most of the larger schools have an office dedicated to posting job opportunities in the surrounding community that may be of interest to students. These can include part-time or full-time positions, short-term positions that offer a flexible schedule or career positions for graduates; and
- Networking – Putting the word out among trusted business colleagues can prove to be a beneficial source of candidates through associations, affiliations, social and service organizations.

3. Conduct An Effective Interview

The third step in the process is an effective and appropriate interview approach. Good practices here are essential to selecting the most qualified candidate while avoiding common mistakes that can have legal implications.

Begin with a list of questions that are job-specific (refer to the job description) and which can help clarify for you (the interviewer), the knowledge, skills, and abilities of the candidate.

Be careful to avoid any questions that seem to imply employment discrimination. A thorough internet search will make clear what types of interview questions should be avoided. For further information, refer to Title VII of the Civil Rights Act of 1964, information provided by the Department of Labor and the Equal Employment Opportunity Commission.

These are a few best practices you should apply for an effective interview:

- give each candidate the same interview experience. (For example: Don't offer a bottle of water to one candidate and take another out to lunch. Don't offer a candidate who made a good impression, a tour of the facility while ushering out the door, another you have concerns about);
- ask the same questions of each interview candidate. This makes comparing and contrasting the candidates fair, consistent and easier to differentiate;
- keep notes of the candidates' responses and rate those responses according to what answer you were expecting from them; and
- consider having one or two other persons from your firm (those who understand the job requirements) join you in the interviews. This approach underscores the validity of a fair hiring process, achieves "buy-in" of the selection decision from the existing staff, and allows you, who will make the final hiring decision, a better understanding of the characteristics of the job that are most important to the people already performing it.

4. Make An Offer

Once you have identified the best-qualified candidate, you still have work to do. Unfortunately, too many employers jump to fill the position, and leave for chance, that they have made a good decision.

After all the effort (and expense) invested to get to the point of making an offer, this may be the most critical time for applying sound fundamentals to the hiring process.

The offer should be in writing and include the following:

- the specific details of the position being offered, such as job title, work location, reporting relationship, employment status (part-time or full-time, seasonal or regular, exempt or non-exempt, etc.) wages, benefits (if any and when eligibility occurs), paid time off, holidays and any the documentation you require the person to bring in to verify their identity and/ or citizenship;

- the offer should include language that clearly stipulates that the offer is contingent upon verification of the information provided, a background check, and possibly a bio-analysis to confirm the candidate is not using illicit drugs;
- such contingencies should include:
  - contacting past employers to verify the time frame and the type of positions that were stated in the interview. Most employers will not offer any details about employee performance and will not share the wages paid unless the employee signs a release of employment information;
  - contacting references provided to confirm they will attest to referenced statements or relationships;
  - contacting schools to verify that the stated education is legitimate;
  - conducting a local (or nation-wide) criminal background check; and
  - contracting with a lab to conduct a bio-analysis (UA).

Some or all of these services can be contracted through service providers but some can also be achieved by simply investing an hour and doing it yourself (except, of course, the drug test which should only be performed by a certified and licensed laboratory).

Take note of E-Verify, a government-provided Internet-based system that compares information required of employees to complete Form I-9 with data from U.S. Department of Homeland Security and Social Security Administration records to confirm employment eligibility. Hosted by the Department of US Citizenship and Immigration Services, it provides a quick and convenient way to verify citizenship status and ensures that employers avoid hiring persons who are ineligible to work in the US.

5. Provide Good Orientation

The final aspect of the recruiting process that assures better selection outcomes and retention is the orientation. Think in terms of what a new employee needs to know to be successful in their job including:

- how to access job-specific training needed to perform their duties;
- the name of the person assigned to provide detailed information about their responsibilities beyond the job description. Who will answer their questions on the first few days on the job?;
- the timing of (90-day, 6-month, annual) and the person responsible for their performance reviews;
- where to find information about company policies and culture, safety requirements, management practices, and reporting relationships;
- where to access needed contact information, for customers both inside and outside the company;
- benefits description and eligibility (if any); and
- an explanation of initial periods related to the position determined.

The recruiting process can result in occasional surprises, even disappointments, because of the human factor. However, when you build discipline and process controls into your recruiting efforts, you will yield more consistent results and return greater value for your investment.

You will also achieve some goodwill with your employees and the candidates they refer when they observe that you have deployed a fair and consistent selection process focused on hiring the most qualified candidates.

COMPENSATION

Pay decisions are often driven by external market conditions. When making employment offers or discussing pay with your employees, you will typically learn what other employers are paying.

Depending on the location of your firm, you may also have to consider minimum wage laws levied by city or state jurisdictions.

It is well outside the scope of this book to offer the information required to assemble a comprehensive compensation plan for your firm. There are, however, several excellent sources for guidance on this subject available through online services such as PayScale.com, Salary.com, and Indeed.com/ Salary Wizard. Many business associations may also offer compensation surveys at discounted rates for members or survey participants.

Regardless of how you arrive at salary decisions, there are a few important points to keep in mind:

1. Compensation decisions must be consistent and fair;

2. Seek to achieve compensation equity based on the scope of responsibilities and contributions; and

3. Performance-based pay is easier to manage, justify and better understood by employees.

The Department of Labor, Wage and Hour Division also provides guidance on such important matters as the Fair Labor Standards Act, the definition of exempt and non-exempt employees, payment of overtime, employee rights, minimum wage, FMLA (The Family and Medical Leave Act of 1993), immigration, pay deductions, wage garnishments, child labor, and many other pay-related topics.

POLICY

Regardless of size, every business should provide employees with access to a set of written policies that outline workplace expectations and define company-provided benefits and conditions. An employee handbook is the most common company approach for policy communication and maintenance. When it is maintained on a shared drive and identified with a revision date, it is easy to keep current and assure employees that they are accessing the most current version.

Employee handbooks should include an Employee Acknowledgement page that allows employees to confirm (with their signature) that they have read, understand and will comply with the contents of the handbook.

This acknowledgment should be retained and reviewed with any employee who strays from that compliance. If an employee handbook seems too cumbersome or excessive, a simple listing of standards or policy statements can be issued periodically to employees and saved to a readily accessible file.

An important point to consider is that employees prefer orderliness in the workplace. Written policies and practices establish expectations and provide employers who write them a firmly stated foundation from which to maintain that order.

EMPLOYMENT PRACTICES INSURANCE

Recently, a small woman-owned employment agency was sued and forced to defend itself against a claim of racial discrimination in a case where it had placed a person into a temporary contract role with another larger employer.

The plaintiff, a minority female, claimed that when the temporary contract position did not result in her placement with the large employer in the regular, full-time position she sought, she had been discriminated against because of her race.

The plaintiff also alleged that the employment agency had assured her that she would get the job. Both the defendants vigorously denied the allegations and were prepared to defend themselves. The large employer, who was also named in the suit, had purchased insurance to cover employment practices. Unfortunately, the employment agency had not.

Eventually, the defendants agreed that it made better sense, from a business perspective, to settle the case rather than expose the defendants to unwanted publicity and the precious time and expense of defending their case.

The employment agency, which had done nothing more than engage in normal business practices, was liable for their portion of the settlement and was forced to secure a business loan to cover legal costs. In the end, this amounted to more than five times what they would have paid for employment practice insurance.

As is true with all insurance, the liability of risk must be weighed on balance with the cost of purchasing insurance coverage to mitigate that risk. A decision not to purchase insurance is, therefore, a decision to self-insure or a decision to accept all legal and financial responsibility for any liability that may be incurred. Small businesses often have general liability protection for most property and casualty circumstances.

You might be well advised to contact your insurance broker to determine the limits of your general liability coverage and whether those limits offer any relief for employment practice matters. If not, you may obtain reasonably priced coverage (which are issued as riders to your policy) to cover employment practices, errors and omissions, and other such protection.

COUNSELING

One of the more important but unsung duties of the HR professional in an organization is to provide employees with counseling support and referrals.

Some in the discipline say that those are the moments that make their job interesting and rewarding. Generally, the kind of person who chooses HR as their profession tends to be endowed with exceptional people skills combined with a "toolbox" filled with help, resources, work experiences, and employment practices.

Whether you retain an abundance of people skills or not, as a small business owner, you can expect that your employees will from time to time seek your guidance on a host of subjects that you will have varying degrees of experience or knowledge in.

A typical list of workplace issues that employees will seek guidance on include:

- absences (pregnancy leave, FMLA, paid time off, personal leave, military leave, etc.);
- accommodations (requests for special consideration pertaining to disability, religion, pregnancy, nursing, parenting, exercise, parking, noise abatement, diet, medical condition, etc.);
- co-worker disagreements;
- discrimination;
- employment law issues (FLSA (Fair Labor Standards Act 1938), FMLA, ADA (Americans with Disabilities Act of 1990), overtime, equal pay, child labor, sick leave, etc.);
- financial challenges;
- flexible schedule;
- forms (I-9, W-2, W-4, ITAR, Emergency Contacts, Change of Address, etc.);
- harassment;
- immigration (visas, green cards, work permits, false identification, etc.);
- nepotism;
- payroll deductions;
- policy questions;
- substance abuse challenges (presented as a confession or discovered through reasonable suspicion);
- transportation challenges (mass transit passes, bicycling, shuttles, commuting delays, etc.);

- workers compensation;
- workplace safety; and
- virtual work.

After reviewing the list above, you may understand the sense of employers choosing to develop and maintain an employee handbook. That said, even the most comprehensive collection of written polices cannot account for every possible scenario that may be raised by employees.

It is absolutely okay to tell your employee that you would like to research the matter they have raised and get back to them. However, before the employee leaves your office, agree on a reasonable date to reconvene to discuss your decision and follow through. Like anything in business, you get better with practice and experience. Don't shy away or ignore your employees. Develop your people skills.

Embrace opportunities to have one-on-one discussions with your employees and consider it one of the best ways to keep your finger on the pulse of your business.

Consider joining your local SHRM (Society of Human Resources Management) Chapter. Meetings are typically held monthly in most major cities, include a sit-down meal and feature guest speakers who provide current and relevant information on a wide range of employment topics.

The meetings are usually attended by HR professionals looking to stay current but also include small business leaders looking to network and gain valuable insight into matters that affect their business. It's a great way to get advice and referrals for the price of admission.

Bill George earned a BA in Health Education from the University of Washington and an MS in Human Resources Management from Chapman University. During his 30 years of leadership within the HR discipline, he has served in a variety of industries and settings including as

a Senior HR Manager for The Boeing Company, an Associate Professor of HR Management in graduate studies for Webster University and as a Vice President of Human Resources for Logistic Specialties Inc. He currently serves as the Director of Human Resources for Skills Inc., a social enterprise in the Boeing supply chain that is a model of an inclusive workforce, providing employment for persons with disabilities as one of the largest suppliers to The Boeing Company in the Puget Sound Region.

References

- Suzanne Lucas in the Inc 2014 article, *5 Signs That You Should Hire an HR Person*;
- Charles Fleischer, *HR for Small Business: An Essential Guide for Managers, Human Resources Professionals, and Small Business Owners (Quick Start Your Business)*, 2009;
- John Putzier and David Baker, *The Everything HR Kit*, 2010;
- Oracle Human Capital, *Modern HR for Dummies*;
- Motor City Books, *Human Resources Kit for Dummies*, 2009;
- Recruiterbox, *9 Great Resources for Human Resources Professionals*, 2012; and
- Berkeley Human Resources, *Guide to Managing Human Resources*, http://hr.berkeley.edu/hr-network.

16 | Did They Board the Right Bus?

Creating effective systems and procedures that support you

Treat employees like they make a difference and they will

–Jim Goodnight, SAS CEO

Through 2006, the economy was booming. Businesses were popping up everywhere as new entrepreneurs took advantage of what appeared to be an ideal condition for easy business success - a rise in income levels, booming construction, and real estate markets, banks lending obscene amounts of money with little creditworthiness, the list goes on. Positioned for growth, my little firm was quickly growing, becoming a competitive and profitable enterprise. This did, however, create a new challenge for me.

LEARNING TO LET GO

In early 2004, my firm consisted of my bookkeeper/receptionist and I. Those were the good old days. Those were the days when I had a complete handle on every aspect of my company – customer service, meeting the clients' daily needs, managing an employee and answering the phone. I knew exactly what needed to be done and I led my staff member through this perfectly. However, by the end of 2005 and into 2006, I was facing a wholly different world, one I had never quite been exposed to before.

> Employees quit or are lured away to better jobs when their expectations are not fulfilled. Meeting these expectations is easy but often, small business owners who work crazy hours tend to overlook them.

Employees needed to be hired and trained. These new staff needed to be managed and led to achieve the objectives of the company. I struggled with having to allow my staff to handle or "touch" client files. Some days, I felt like there was nobody steering this ship anymore. Other days, I felt like I had an overloaded ship struggling to get into port.

There was also the issue of turnover. Was there anyone who was interested in holding a job, doing an honest day's work, on coming in on time, on having pride in good work and maybe, just maybe, taking a little initiative in serving the customers?

Luckily for me, I hired a coach who not only knew how to help my company market itself well, he also knew how to train me to lead my team. Truth be told, if I had simply listened to him every step of the way, the headaches would have been few and far between.

Had I been willing to delegate, to empower my staff, to diligently provide training and clear systems for them to follow, we would have avoided some of the turnover, retained a few more clients and the resulting growth would have been much higher.

AN EFFECTIVE HIRING PROCESS

One of the first systems I adopted from my coach is the Four Step Hiring Process. This process took a lot of time to implement but compared to my previous system of "gut feel" combined with "hopefully, she is competent and a good fit for our company", I gradually developed a highly successful system for attracting and hiring the staff I wanted.

This Four-Step Hiring Process is outlined below.

THE FOUR STEP HIRING PROCESS

Step 1 - Recruit the right people.

Step 2 - Pre-screen and select the right candidate for the interview.

Step 3 - Conduct a three-step interview process.

Step 4 - Select and hire the best.

Visit www.smallbizzoom.com to download the full kit (process, tools, and resources.

RETAINING GOOD PEOPLE

Once we began to get the right people on our bus, the next step was to train and retain them, if desired. The first step in this process of creating a winning package consisted of compensation and benefits, providing a friendly and fun working environment, and accountability.

Employees quit or are lured away to better jobs when their expectations are not fulfilled. Meeting these expectations is easy but often, small business owners who work crazy hours tend to overlook them. Develop a detailed retention program that includes the following, and then, put a well-intentioned staff member in charge of ensuring it is followed consistently.

DEVELOPING AN EMPLOYEE RETENTION PROGRAM

1. Implement the Four-Step Hiring Process making sure your entire team is involved.

2. Develop a system for holding each employee accountable for the responsibilities outlined in their Positional Contract.

3. Develop company policies and put together an Employee Manual.

4. Develop a complete "How To" manual for every job in your company.

5. Develop an Employee Induction Program which includes detailed training on your company policies, various job functions and your system of accountability.

6. Conduct regular relationship-building activities including team-building events:

   a. birthday parties, company client retention parties or just simply, parties; and

   b. weekly or monthly (brief) team meetings.

7. Develop team Bonus Programs. Ensure that it is measurable and make it an "All Team Wins" event.

Sometime in March 2005, I faced a little crisis. I was already implementing these procedures within my company. We were continually adding new clients to the firm who needed attention but I had yet to create a solid employee retention program.

Three key employees walked off with no notice, leaving a gaping hole. I couldn't get both the payroll tax and federal income tax filings completed in a timely manner. I had to get the work done quickly.

I needed to hire a few more new staff urgently. I had to conduct training and there was just not enough time to get all of this done. With tax deadlines looming, I decided to hire the most experienced payroll person I could find. I was going to handle all the taxes personally.

Three interviews in, I met Patricia. She was happy to take on the payroll work. She was knowledgeable enough to do this. Then I shared a little bit about my dilemma and she informed me that she might be able to serve me better as a tax preparer because she had more than 20 years of experience in this area. My gut reaction - not a chance! When I updated my business coach about it, he scolded me, quickly convincing me that I should let her do the taxes.

We had two weeks left of the tax season and four weeks left to do payroll. Despite the unspoken fear of potential audits and angry clients, I relented and went to work on payroll. I caught up on where things were and then managed to also create a complete "How To" manual for the payroll person, hired someone great for the position, trained them and then went through a complete audit of all our records to make sure everything was fine. All the while, I watched quietly in the background, as Patricia started meeting with our clients and completing the work I had started.

On 1 May, after both the tax and payroll deadlines, Patricia asked me to sit down with her and review a few things, which I was happy to do. She shared details of all the returns she had completed and told me about several customer compliments received, which was great. However, she then went on to quiz me about two tax returns I had done, contending that they were not only incorrect but that one of them needed immediate attention to avoid an IRS audit!

My first thought was to tell her who the boss was and take a hard stand defending my actions. Luckily, I quickly defused that spark of arrogance. I listened as she spoke, looked at the details closely, and after she was done, all but gave this sweet lady a bear hug!

When you are able to find and surround yourself with people smarter than you, your team wins big.

This was only the beginning.

Patricia had spent years managing employees. As soon as I saw her in action, teaching my new payroll hire how to be even better, she was promoted instantly to office manager. The groundwork was in place now for team development, a bonus program and accountability for the entire team.

For the next several months, as the company continued to grow, Patricia and I implemented many great tactics such as continuous training of our staff, an awesome scoreboard measuring team successes, employee fun activities, all of which led to a very successful year. Anybody can achieve the same in their own business.

Take the time to implement these systems and procedures in your company and begin getting the right people on your bus. As you do this, you may encounter some hires who just do not work out. However, if you can recognize they are simply on the wrong bus, you can take action to remove, and then replace them. Fire fast and hire slow, and your team will steadily grow.

End of Chapter Action Items

1. **Work on your hiring process**

   Visit www.smallbizzoom.com to download the "Four-Step Hiring Process". As you prepare to hire your next employee, document in detail the new process for all future hiring activities. Then, check out other hiring and training resources available on our website.

2. **Create Positional Contracts**

   Do this for every position in your company. Consult ActionCoach for more about creating positional contracts – www.smallbizzoom.com

3. **Review retention procedures**

   Review the list of Retention Procedures I provided above. Once this plan is created, select a member of your team who will implement each aspect of the plan and the intended outcomes.

4. **Document processes**

   Have each team member create a detailed "How To" manual for all of the individual responsibilities of their position. Why should you do this? Should an employee depart suddenly or without notice, a new hire will be able to fulfill his role, guided entirely by what is captured in the manual.

5. **Create an Employee Review System**

   Ensure that it includes accountability to the company's Vision, Mission and Goals, along with the employee's Positional Contract. Include a formula each employee agrees upon to determine their bonuses and raises.

6. **Measure success**

   Consider the ways in which your team, as a whole, works to create the company's success each year. Develop a way to measure each team member's success and begin measuring this on a large scoreboard visible to all team members. Create a specific bonus program, that is inclusive, for all employees working together to achieve measurable success. Then, create milestones and celebrate successes along the way.

7. **Create your job description as the business owner.**

   Determine at what volume of activity and at what date, you will hire individuals to systematically take over key roles within your company, such as bookkeeping, sales and marketing, operations, human resources and quality assurance. As part of this process, identify the Key Performance Indicators (expected measurable outcomes) by which you will measure the results of each position.

17 | Surround Yourself with Greatness

A network of influence, skill and expertise - *your* network

If you want to go somewhere, it is best to find someone who has already been there

–Robert Kiyosaki

U ntil I read *The 21 Irrefutable Laws of Leadership: Follow Them and People Will Follow You* by John C. Maxwell, I considered myself a solo-entrepreneur. If it was to be, it was up to me!

After I read this book, I envisioned and then created the environment and processes at the office to empower my team to solve our daily problems. The results were more profound than I could have ever expected.

My team at the office have (and know that they have), the power to identify and solve almost every problem that comes along. They are more engaged and dedicated as a result. Coming to work became more fun and challenging. Retention continues to be high. This was, however, only the beginning. On three occasions, while operating my CPA firm, I have been involved in the acquisition and management of other companies.

This is not easy. However, when you have an office that works as a team, solving most problems with little or no involvement from me as the owner, then the idea of acquiring and operating other companies becomes possible.

> If you want to move to the next level in life and your business, if you want better resources that you can bounce your ideas off of, if you want connections to a wider network, then you need to take the time to identify Power Partners.

Doing this requires effective communication and detailed Key Performance Indicators that are monitored closely so as to catch problems as they arise. Additionally, for your business to run successfully without your active and day to day involvement as an owner, requires wisdom, skills and talents greater than your own.

CREATE YOUR DREAM TEAM

I credit much of my business success to having surrounded myself with a team of Power Partners with specialized talents and skills better than my own. I work with this close team of individuals who help me succeed and I do the same for them.

For example, I have shared with my clients many experiences involving my business coach. His skills in making a business highly profitable are far superior to my own. Consequently, he has teamed up to help more than 200 of my clients achieve similar business successes.

Another invaluable Power Partner to me has been my business attorney. He has kept me out of trouble many times, given me great tips and tools to avoid potential disasters and assisted me in providing services to many hundreds of my business clients.

Additionally, I have two close colleagues who are highly successful entrepreneurs. They share their success strategies, provide connections to me and bring me loads of new business all the time.

I have created a Power Partner team of six individuals to date. Without any of them, my business and career path would not be close to what it is today. Consider also that a CPA may be a good partner to have because such a person likely has practical business, accounting, tax and consulting experience.

If you want to move to the next level in life and your business, if you want better resources that you can bounce your ideas off of, if you want connections to a wider network, then you need to take the time to identify Power Partners. These could be people who are within your current circle or people who you could approach.

Invite them to meet with you and begin sharing your goals and listening to theirs. This is the start of your Power Partnership which will help you become a better businessperson, better leader, and hopefully, boost your business even further.

End of Chapter Action Items

1. **Create your Power Partners Now**

   Take the first step. Schedule a lunch or meeting with one or two individuals who you think can help you and who you can help too.

18 | Lead the Way

Building a company requires solid leadership, a clear and engaging mission and the skills and experience to lead your people forward

The task of the leader is to get his people from where they are to where they have not been

–Henry Kissinger

When I first started my business, I thought I was someone really big. I was self-employed, independent, and by luck, I started off profitably from day one. The reality, though, was that I was green, inexperienced and completely lacking in the knowledge and insight needed to give my clients what they wanted and what they were paying me for.

BECOMING THE LEADER YOU NEED TO BE

I was what was referred to as a Level 1 leader (borrowed from John C. Maxwell's concept of five levels of leadership in his book, *The Five Levels of Leadership: Proven Steps to Maximize Your Potential*). I was the owner and the boss; employees answered to me and respected my title but they did not necessarily respect me.

For the first five years, I would "control" my business from this paradigm, without even realizing it. I did not understand, even with the external help of a business coach, why I had huge turnover and unhappy employees.

It wasn't until I had the amazing opportunity to take a microscopic lens to my blind spots that things began to change. I attended the Landmark Forum one weekend, through www.landmarkeducation.com, and those three days forever changed who I was to other people. (I highly recommend this program for anyone seeking better relationships or trying but not succeeding in letting go of the past!).

With this, I was able to then step up to become a Level 2 leader. My staff accept me as their leader. Mutual respect, commitment and integrity are the foundations we naturally live by. We work together, in an environment where the weaknesses of team members are compensated by the strengths of other team members. We work in such a way that, as a team, we are able to meet deadlines and serve our stakeholders.

Building on this solid foundation, we began setting very challenging team goals for growth and success within the firm (not to mention the successes of the teams of other businesses).

Level 3 in leadership is about bringing a team together to work synergistically to achieve great success. We set goals to double our growth while simultaneously providing all of our clients with the support and resources they needed to succeed. Consequently, we have achieved several years of powerful success as a company and as a team.

Where are you at in terms of these leadership levels? Do you feel like you have to be a micromanager in order to achieve success? Are you new to leading a team? Or do you feel confident that mutual respect, team commitment and integrity lead your team's daily interactions? If the latter, congratulations!

This is a long, hard process and it requires a high degree of self-discipline and much relationship building with your team.

Perhaps you have successfully helped your team achieve seemingly unachievable goals whereby your teamwork has created a "1 + 1 = 3" type equation (or maybe more!) simply because synergy creates that outcome.

Success in business does not happen by accident. It is not about having more money than your competitor nor is it about being a technician great at providing your clients with the services or products they want.

Success in business comes from leading yourself and others in the mastery of the strategies outlined in this book. It is about striving for such mastery consistently, relentlessly and with a keen eye on measurable success.

WHAT HIGHLY EFFECTIVE PEOPLE DO

The 7 Habits of Highly Effective People: Powerful Lessons in Personal Change by Stephen R Covey is an excellent framework for this purpose. This book is a must-read for people in any kind of leadership or entrepreneurial role. Reading both Covey's and this book fulfills Covey's first habit: Be Proactive.

The next habit is "Begin with the End in Mind" which, for me, translates as setting measurable goals for success. ActionCoach provides a formula for setting any goal, outlined below.

SMART GOALS

Specific - clearly identify your goal;

Measurable - clearly identify how it will be considered accomplished;

Attainable - ensure you can actually achieve it. How will you say, "I did it"?;

Relevant - how will this goal help you reach your greater Vision, Mission, Objectives and other goals?

Timely - when, in time and action, will it be considered complete?

When you begin measuring success, it becomes a palpable reality. Let me explain. When I was 16 years old, I bought my first car, a beautiful El Camino. I had not realized that, at the time, my goal to own this car started six months previously on the day I received my driver's permit. My uncle who owned an old El Camino allowed me to sit in the driver's seat one day and he then gave me the car keys. We drove for a few miles and I was hooked!

After that, I began to notice hundreds of El Caminos all over town. I had no idea it was such a popular car. It wasn't actually. It was just my brain's reticular activating system at play. Six months later I was driving my own El Camino – as proud as a dad with his first child in his arms.

When you set goals, the reticular activating system goes off in your brain. With the repeated review of your goals, you begin to imagine and then plan and implement ways to realize these goals.

Setting goals is one thing. Achieving them, however, takes something else. I wrote earlier about setting seven daily tasks that all work towards reaching the goals you set.

This is a habit that Covey refers to, in his book, as "putting first things first" - this is key to success. When you focus and execute on the highest priorities in any goal or plan you have, magic occurs.

You then notice you are making marked progress as well as completing the little activities that ultimately complete your goals, all of which work towards your Vision and Mission.

I find the second half of Covey's book to be particularly good. Here, he talks about communicating effectively. This is when you listen twice as much as you speak so that you are able to fully understand the other person's viewpoint.

You also create win/win situations for all company stakeholders and you work as a team to achieve your company's mission and goals.

When this happens, everything begins to shift, you feel the synergy and a giant leap forward is made.

SUCCESS PATHWAY

No matter your level of success, continued growth can be achieved by embracing principles of leadership, educating yourself continuously, creating measurable goals, working with great power partners who challenge and inspire you, and with a coach or otherwise, being accountable to reach your Vision.

With insights learned from *The Ultimate Sales Machine* by Chet Holmes, I implemented a daily activity of completing seven tasks daily, every day.

With the training and accountability, I get from my business coach, I have set and achieved hundreds of goals over the years. The combination of these has produced massive results beyond any measure! You can do the same.

At first, all these goals and dreams were more for personal gratification. I made money and achieved great things. Today, it is very different. I find it a great joy now to recognize that I am paying it forward by giving back to my clients, employees and other business stakeholders, my family and spouse, my church and my community.

A VISION OF THE FUTURE

So, ask yourself this question: What is your vision for yourself and your future?

As Stephen Covey put it, in his great book, *The 7 Habits of Highly Effective People*, imagine yourself at your own funeral. What are your family and friends, colleagues and the community going to say about you? What will their speech be? Today, you have the ability to influence, almost write, these speeches about yourself. So, what is your vision, who are you and what do you want to be in this short life we share?

Create for yourself a bucket list of goals, things you would like to achieve in this life, no matter your age or circumstances. Think big and small. Write it all down and keep this list in your possession - whether on your electronic device or on your bathroom mirror. When I was 16 years old, I created a list of 100-lifetime goals. I have achieved 68 of these so far and made progress on many others.

Next, create your Vision. Create a statement on paper that will truly inspire you day after day, year after year, to be the person you most desire to be. This is my vision today. Yes, it could change but this is what it is today.

> **My Vision**
> Be a nationally sought-after public speaker, successful entrepreneur and author. Inspire a million people.

Next, if your company's Vision and Mission Statements do not exist, you should also do the same here. Then establish annual and five-year goals for your business that you review regularly with your team.

Share all of this with your team. Perhaps even create it with them as you want your team to buy into your vision, the mission for achieving it and then work together to achieve those goals.

WHY SPEND TIME ON DEVELOPING YOUR VISION AND MISSION

A Vision gives a company the destination. A Mission defines the map (or direction), key processes and the ways in which you shall reach your Vision. With a Vision and Mission, you have the end in mind.

Now, create the 10 - 20 milestones that will get you to your Vision. Some of these milestones will be within the next few months. Others will be within the next few years or decades. Yet, you need to define what you will do, abiding by your Mission Statement, in order to achieve your Vision.

A SHORT STORY

In the 1300s, at Cambridge University in England, a chapel was constructed for one of the colleges. The enormous roof was supported by huge beams created from old-growth oak.

Seven hundred years later, the beams had deteriorated so much that the roof was in danger of collapsing.

The building required extensive renovation, including replacement of the beams. But where, in the present day, could those tasked with repairing the building find giant oak trees of such an age and quality as had been available to the original builders?

The answer lay right outside the chapel door. The original builders of the chapel had known that, at some point far in the future, the structure would need new oak beams. So, they had planted acorns in the churchyard. Over the centuries, a grove of oak trees had grown to full maturity.

Vision is all about creating the future. Create a future in your company that provides for the success of all shareholders.

BECOME A POWERFUL INFLUENCER

To achieve your Vision, you must be able to influence and motivate your stakeholders.

These may include many types of people including:

- family members involved, at any level, in the success of you and your business;
- employees, both your own, as well as those of the other companies you work with;
- vendors and customers with whom you do business;
- professionals who are directly involved in your success – bankers, coaches, accountants, etc;

- the Government – in fact, there are times where influencing government employees could be more critical than anyone else for a number of reasons; and
- prospective customers – whether directly or indirectly, you need to influence them to buy from you.

Your ability to effectively influence the actions of many of these stakeholders is what will determine your success in business. Period.

So, how can you be more influential? Here are a few powerful ways to make an impact, persuade, negotiate, communicate with and otherwise influence others in business.

Reciprocation

I am obligated to give back to you the attitude you gave me. You give to me and I must give to you. If I do you a favor, you owe me a favor. People say yes to those they owe.

The questions to ask are: Who can I help? Whose outcomes can I improve here?

Be the first to give. An example: A server at a restaurant increases the number of tips he receives if he puts a piece of candy on the tray. Two mints multiply his results. If someone receives something unexpectedly beneficial to them, they will likely give you more in return.

Scarcity

In most things, there is a limited amount of resources available. You may be the only one selected to work here. You may have a limited supply of inventory. You may provide, through your product/service/idea, something that others cannot get from your competitors. Point to the feature(s) they can't get anywhere else.

Authority

This is not about being "in authority", as in possessing power and control. Rather, it is about being "an authority" as in being recognized as knowledgeable, competent and an expert on an issue. In essence, you are providing a shortcut or a way forward through a maze. An example: As the author of a book, you often become an automatic authority on the subject you speak about.

Admitting weakness FIRST

In terms of any product or service offered, there are always two elements in the mind of your audience or prospective customer – your expertise and trustworthiness. One way to gain trustworthiness is to mention a weakness in your case or a drawback to your argument before you present the strongest elements. It builds trustworthiness because you will both be providing all the positives and providing a balanced perspective, helping them see the whole picture. Your listener will then feel that they need to listen to what you have to say.

Consistency

People want to see you as consistent with what you present as if you are aligned with what you offer. You do not want to appear confused or dishonest in what you present.

Recognize that, often, people *want to appear* to be consistent in their activities, opinions, behaviors, and attitudes. If you ask them to take a small step in your direction, going towards the larger picture or vision, you need to make it appear that it is consistent with what they are already doing.

An example: Let's say that you have an employee who is not doing an aspect of their job correctly but they are acting as a team player. Build the team player's strength up and share how others on that team are successful in completing this aspect of their job and how they could do the same as well.

Consensus

Provide information about how others just like them are doing what is needed. "Others in this very hotel are reusing their towels." Don't go against the grain or be unique when consensus wins. An example: This team is succeeding as X, Y and Z. It is achievable and you are a part of a powerful team.

Liking

Show a preference for saying *yes* to those you know and like. Share information about yourself that shows how you are similar and have common goals and comparable purposes. Give honest praise. An example: I shared with you my epilepsy story, and many other stories, in order to build trust with you as to my character.

Rarely does anyone achieve automatic influence, it must be cultivated. Using the elements and situations above can draw people toward you and create a situation of influence. Here are a few other things you might consider doing to become more influential:

1. Before getting into a situation calling for a display of influence, take a step back and review what's available for you to show you are influential here. Are you an expert? Is there a unique feature you can provide that your competitors do not possess? Do you have testimonials that can back your claims?

2. Always speak or act first so that people want to listen to what you have to offer. People aren't willing to take much time to listen.

> You determine the success of your business.
> You determine the level at which your team turns
> your goals, Mission and Vision into a reality.

3. Use multiple tactics to influence others. There is no single tactic that is all-important. Together, they present a powerful force.

4. Cast your Vision often. It is about being consistent and building consensus among your team players.

5. Be authentic in every interaction. Authenticity is what attracts people to you. This is about being consistent but may also be about admitting a weakness first, at times.

THE LEADERSHIP EVALUATION

When the grind continues on day after day in business, and you feel that you are inevitably stuck "working in" your business (when you'd much rather be "working on" it), leadership is the key. Taking it a step further, if you implement a culture of leadership in your company, you begin to create leaders who will propel you to new levels of success.

The Maxwell Leadership Game

Creating a culture of leadership in your business doesn't have to be a stress-filled process of disrupting routines and demanding, or begging for, compliance. It can be achieved by learning principles of leadership as a team, as a game.

The Maxwell Leadership Game is a fun, engaging way to bring people together and teach leadership principles while growing as a team and providing education. Check out this game on our website at www.smallbizzoom.com if you're looking for a great tool to begin developing your team into leaders.

Leadership is about developing influence. In business, leadership is about the ability to share your Vision, Mission, and goals with your team in such a way that you inspire and empower them to help you fulfill your Vision. How effective are you at inspiring and empowering your employees to achieve your business objectives?

Establish your goals. Be specific about them. Add to your list the goals suggested by your peers. There is a law of leadership that many do not realize or understand: whatever level of leadership you attain, it presents the limit at which you will lead others towards achievement. As the leader of your business, you are at the top. Others will not remain under your employ if they feel that they are a better leader than you. Likewise, the people you employ will not be comfortable staying and feeling that they're a better leader than you are.

You determine the success of your business. You determine the level at which your team turns your goals, Mission and Vision into reality. You determine the level at which synergy, or lack thereof, occurs. You determine the level at which teamwork is developed, cultivated, fostered or achieved in your business.

You are the leader. Develop your leadership and you accelerate the rate at which success is achieved. Remain stagnant or decline and you then watch success trickle to eventual business failure.

Everything rises or falls on the ability to lead and influence others. This refers to and includes your customers, vendors, family and colleagues because everyone contributes towards your success.

So, begin implementing a plan to develop your level of leadership so that you can guarantee the accomplishment of your business Vision, Mission, and goals. When you need help developing the process, remember that we have an entire academy of resources to assist you.

The Business Success Academy

Some of you may read this book and use it to fill every hole in your business. Others may need a program or an organized system to follow. You need good leaders and experts to help you reach the pinnacle of success in your business and to become the leader you desire to be. To this end, we have created this exclusive webinar series called The Business Success Academy to help you achieve massive success.

The Business Success Academy includes six months of personalized, business-focused webinars, one-on-one coaching from a certified ActionCOACH and training directly from many of the world's leading entrepreneurs who want you to succeed.

When you sign up for the Academy, you become a member for life with full access to our resources. Organize your strategies for success. Take a five-year leap forward in business success today. Get insights from top business coaches and many highly successful entrepreneurs. Visit www.smallbizzoom.com to sign up today.

You've created your business path. Now let's turn it into the most successful business in your industry!

PAY IT FORWARD

As you complete these tasks with the end in mind, it is likely that some of this may be focused on 'paying it forward'. You will have goals, a vision and a mission, that as you live them out will enrich the lives of your team, your family, your community and colleagues.

There is great power that comes from investing in the success of others that you may not expect. Commonly referred to as the law of reciprocity, you will find that others will return the favor as you 'pay it forward'.

In the process of carrying out these activities, you will begin to create your future. From there, you can focus and execute on your highest priorities day by day, year by year. You can utilize the many tools and resources in this book, from marketing to tax, business or personal tips, to become a successful business owner and successful at life. In the process, you may also find yourself able to help others achieve similar successes.

End of Chapter Action Items

1. **Required reading**

   - John C. Maxwell's *The Five Levels of Leadership: Proven Steps to Maximize Your Potential;*
   - Stephen R Covey's *The 7 Habits of Highly Effective People: Powerful Lessons in Personal Change.*

2. **Register for the next Landmark Forum**

   To attain independence for yourself, for freedom from the past and to identify your blind spots in life, attend this Forum.

3. **Work on the following for your business**

   a. a Vision Statement;

   b. a Mission Statement;

   c. five or more long-term goals and financial projections;

   d. a few annual goals;

   e. goals from the 90-day Plan for each quarter; and

   f. develop seven daily mini-goals each morning in order to work towards your goals.

4. **Create the following for yourself**

   a. a Vision Statement;

   b. a Family Mission Statement; and

   c. a bucket list of things you would like to accomplish in your life.

5. **Work on becoming influential**

   Review all the examples of being influential that are outlined in this chapter. Select a technique that suits you well and begin implementing it. Then, teach this technique to other employees. Repeat this process until being influential becomes a habit.

Epilogue

Well, there you have them - the Seven Strategies of Highly Successful Business Owners. Learn them, take them to heart and apply them in your business and life. If you follow these seven core strategies, success in business will follow you!

It is my goal as the author of this book to see that you succeed. This is the reason behind my development of the webinar series, The Business Success Academy.

Many have asked me what specifically I have done in business, as well as in life, to be where I am today. First and foremost, it was not all me. There are many, in my life, who I have shared with you, who are credited for my successes. In addition to their gracious contributions, there have been a few things which have been key to my success:

1. Finding the one thing/solution or ultimate win/win that will give my clients success (or in the case of this book, seven things);

2. Hiring a business coach, and with him, fully implementing the "5 Ways Marketing Formula" across all my businesses consistently for 15 years;

3. Though I did not expect nor hope for this initially, writing this book has brought recognition, trust and a position of authority to everything I do;

4. Outsourcing, streamlining and automating parts of my businesses have multiplied profits fivefold;

5. Building relationships of trust and giving back to my customers has created an incredible referral feast for years;

6. Implementing principles of leadership, influence, and trust have altogether changed the landscape of how I do business. It draws employees, clients and other stakeholders in as they want to be a part of what we are creating.

As you build your organization, remember:

- people determine the potential of your organization;
- the morale of your organization is determined by the relationships you cultivate;
- structure, systems, and procedures determine the size of your organization;
- vision (shared and lived) creates the direction of your organization; and
- leadership determines the level of success in your organization.

I wish you great business success. Pursue your dreams. As my business coach frequently teaches, set and achieve your HAG (Hairy Audacious Goal).

Think big! Put a goal out there that would, if achieved, be the ultimate measure of your success. Then, dig in. Establish long-term milestones and using you PHD, measure your progress towards that HAG. Identify the SMART goals necessary to reach the milestones and so on.

Success in business is not gifted to us. It is planned, implemented, revised, re-evaluated, reorganized, reported on, tested and measured. And then, it is achieved.

MY TOP 15 TAX TIPS
FOR THE SMALL BUSINESS OWNER

Tip #1 Business Health Insurance Tax Credit

Claim the maximum possible Small Business Health Insurance Tax Credit of up to 50 percent of premiums paid for staff health insurance coverage purchased through an exchange. File amended business returns for the three years prior to if the credit was missed or miscalculated.

Tip #2 Find Ways to Deduct Auto Expenses

The best deduction, for nearly all kinds of businesses, is mileage. The exception is when you buy a very expensive vehicle or when you have a large truck with very low mileage on it. If you decide to claim actual expenses rather than mileage, one way you can substantiate the deduction is to "wrap" your car ie decorate your car with your business advertisements. Check your cell phone App Store for cool apps that can help you keep track of all business miles traveled.

Tip #3 Claim the Home Office Deduction

This is a realistic deductible expense for many home businesses even if you do not work exclusively from home or if you only use a space within the home exclusively for your business. Calculating the correct percentage is critical especially if your business is incorporated but many claim the standard deduction of $1,500. If this applies to you, do not fear. Claim this deduction.

Tip #4 File Your Return to Claim a Refund

It amazes me how many do not file a return for long periods of time. They end up losing a refund if this was due to them. The statute of limitations is three years. So, if you have a refund coming to you (or think you might), then complete your tax return to receive it. It's like free money at that point.

Tip #5 Deduct Miles for Charitable Activities

When itemizing deductions on your return, remember whether there was any mileage in conjunction with charitable events. Keep a record of it. Check your cell phone App Store for ways to keep track of charitable miles driven.

Tip #6 Deduct Non-Cash Contributions

The IRS requires special forms for taking non-cash contributions over $500. If you have a lot of items that you have donated, there are several excellent software packages you can use to document these to get fair-market value for them. You can then put this deduction on your Schedule A and have the backup records you need to support you.

Tip #7 Take the Maximum Sec 179 Deduction

Take advantage of the use of the Section 179 Deduction, which is fully depreciating, or writing off new or used equipment purchases. The deductible amount changes each year. There is also, in addition to this, bonus depreciation and then standard depreciation.

Tip #8 Deduct Travel and Other Expenses You Are Required to Pay If Work Related

If you are required to:-

a) use your vehicle for work activities (excluding traveling back and forth from work to home);

b) use your own equipment (eg, computer, cell phone or home office);

c) purchase items (like specialized clothing or professional licenses, etc) for employment, then determine if you qualify for this deduction as part of Form 2106 on Schedule A.

Tip #9 Deduct Your Per Diems

If your profession requires overnight travel and living expenses that you are responsible for paying, you may be eligible for a deduction for per diems - expenses for travel, meals, and lodging. This could be a significant deduction for those who work away from home.

Tip #10 Maximize deductions to your Retirement Plan

Whether you have an IRA, a SEP-IRA, an Owner 401K, a Safe-Harbor 401K, a Solo-401K, a pension plan, or any other kind of qualified plan, make the maximum contribution. This can benefit you in multiple ways:

1) Your contribution directly offsets taxable income;

2) You still have the money. It is just reserved for a more pleasant retirement;

3) Your employer (or your own business, if self-employed) may be able to make contributions to your plan completely tax-free to you;

4) You might be eligible for a tax credit for contributions made. Make higher contributions if you are aged 55 or older.

Tip #11 You Are Always Eligible for A One-Time Waiver of Penalty

If you owe the IRS money, take note that they offer a one-time waiver of penalty that you are eligible for, regardless of your circumstances. If you find one IRS agent denying you this option, go to another. The same holds true for a business – a business is eligible for a one-time waiver of penalty, regardless of what it was incurred for.

Tip #12 The IRS Will Settle Your Debt Under Certain Circumstances

The IRS provides an option for an Offer In Compromise. If you owe the IRS taxes that you believe you are unable to pay, you may go through this process and make them an "Offer" to settle the debt. It is a complicated process, but with our help, it can be completed fairly easily. If you are in this position, you need to get professional advice because it could benefit you to the tune of hundreds or thousands of dollars. Schedule a meeting today either by calling our office at (253) 288-8829 or book this through our website at www.actiontaxteam.com/schedule-now/

If you do not qualify for an Offer, as in the case where you still make some income and wherein the IRS believes they can get paid the taxes due through the garnishment of your bank accounts, you will need to file paperwork with them to set a reasonable payment plan up.

Tip #13 Self-Employed Health Insurance Deduction

If you are self-employed and pay for health insurance, you may be able to deduct premiums paid during the year. This may include the cost to cover your children under age 27 even if they are not your dependents. Look at IRS Publication 535, Business Expenses, for more details.

Tip #14 100% Depreciation for SUV's

Purchase an SUV rated at 6,000 pounds or more fully loaded to be eligible for the $25,000 expensing election (if business use is at least 50%), and 50% bonus deprecation if restored after the election is taken.

Tip #15 Rent residence for tax-free Income

Increase tax-free income by renting your personal residence or vacation home for up to 14 days each year. If not otherwise rented, rent your personal residence and vacation home to shareholders, staff members, staff training and retreats and business meetings. Tax-deductible for the business, tax-free to you.

About the Author

Jacob M Hanes is a public speaker, CPA and entrepreneur. Jake delivers high energy messages that motivate people to take action in life to build highly successful businesses.

As an entrepreneur, he has been coaching business owners for more than 14 years in every facet of operating and growing their business. He has succeeded, as well as failed, in business. He shares his experiences as well as relevant concepts and tools you can use to take a five-year leap in your business success.

Jake lived the first 40 years of his life with epilepsy, enduring thousands of seizures. Yet, amid all the inherent challenges, he reached great heights, including summiting the five highest peaks in Washington and building several successful businesses.

Now cured of epilepsy, he continues to succeed by goal setting and achieving every day. As a CPA and entrepreneur, he takes education very seriously, bringing his challenging experiences to life in educating and entertaining audiences of all sizes.

A graduate of Central Washington University with a BA in Accounting, Jake is a Certified Public Accountant operating a highly successful CPA firm in Auburn, WA. Jake can be contacted at jake@smallbizzoom.com or jhanes@actiontaxteam.com

https://www.linkedin.com/company/action-tax-service-llc

https://twitter.com/actiontaxexpert

https://www.facebook.com/ActionTaxExpert/

Made in the USA
San Bernardino, CA
19 January 2020